FIVE CONTEMPLATIONS BY THICH NHAT HANH

This food is a gift of the whole universe: the earth, the sky, numerous living beings and much hard, loving work.

May we eat with mindfulness and gratitude so as to be worthy to receive this food.

May we recognize and transform our unwholesome mental formations, especially our greed, and learn to eat with moderation.

May we keep our compassion alive by eating in such a way that reduces the suffering of living beings, stops contributing to climate change, and heals and preserves our precious planet.

We accept this food so we may nurture our loved ones, strengthen our community, and nourish our ideal of serving all living beings.

PLANT-BASED INDIAN

COOKBOOK

FREE OF

OIL | SUGAR | DAIRY | GLUTEN

MALA BARUA | NANDINI GULATI

PHOTOGRAPHS
Anand Mohapatra

FOOD STYLING
Mala Barua | Vidhi Jain

Plant-based Indian Cookbook

2022

Tara Press-India Research Press
Flat. 6, Khan Market, New Delhi - 110 003
Ph: 24694610; Fax : 24618637
www.indiaresearchpress.com
contact@indiaresearchpress.com

ISBN 13 : 978-81-8386-201-1

Printed and Bound in India

CONTENTS

FOREWORD

Ms. Maneka Sanjay Gandhi

Former Minister, Ministry of Women and Child Development

One of our 33,000 divinities in India is Shakambhari, Goddess of Hampi, Karnataka. Every year, on her festival day, she is offered 63 vegetables. They probably have a checklist coming down the centuries because I have yet to find someone who can name that many vegetables offhand. Sadly, we have stopped paying attention to our vegetables and old varieties of grains and seeds. We had over 90,000 varieties of rice in 1960. We now have only 23,000 varieties. Once we had long red bhindi (okra). No one has seen it for the last 50 years.

I would like to think that India is still largely vegetarian. But the problem is that people mistake drinking milk to be vegetarianism. If the meat of a cow is non-vegetarian, how can milk from the same animal body be vegetarian? It is for this reason that milk drinkers get the same diseases as meat-eaters – gout, heart disease, cancer, obesity, kidney failure, diabetes… to name a few!

Cows and buffaloes in India, as in most of the world, are riddled with disease. They have been mutated into milk machines and most of them suffer from cancers, leukaemia (Bovine Leukosis Virus or BLV), mastitis, foot and mouth disease, pneumonia, ketosis, brucellosis etc. and are kept alive on antibiotics. I use the word 'most' because it is true in over 70-80% cases. All these diseases are zoonotic – which means drinking their milk could make you vulnerable. In fact, scientific studies have repeatedly shown the presence of BLV cells in women's breast cancer, for instance.

All these animals are given a daily injection of oxytocin, which is a hormone not only to extract the milk faster but which enters the blood and milk stream of the animal. This can cause in humans, everything from early puberty to breast, uterine and prostate cancers, bad eyesight, an imbalance in hair production and more. Milk has been directly related to cancers and diabetes.

The human body is simply not designed to absorb meat or milk. Unlike carnivores, we don't have canines, claws or slit-eyes with wider vision. Our intestines are too long to eliminate meat easily and our saliva is not acidic. All babies cry when introduced to non-mother's milk and their burps become smelly. Every child has to be threatened into drinking milk – because the body rejects the idea and it knows best.

Most of these ailments can be reversed through a healthy vegan diet. Doctors in the West have already started a movement in reversing lifestyle diseases through a 'whole food plant-based' diet. Ayurveda is a fully researched branch of science that does the same.

Unfortunately, in India people tend to believe allopathic doctors who know very little about diet since the essential science of food and its impact on the human body is not included in the curriculum of medical schools. When a doctor, or even a dietician, orders that an ulcer patient should have a glass of cold milk, he will do so not knowing that milk turns to acid in the stomach and will eventually enlarge the ulcer.

Meat eating has been made aspirational - just as smoking and drinking beer was in the 1950s. Cooking shows on TV glorify meat and fish dishes. International chefs often scoff at vegetarian food (except if there is cheese or *paneer* in it) as being boring. However, if you would take a survey of their health issues, most of them will have high blood pressure, high cholesterol, a narrowing of the arteries and almost all of them are overweight.

You don't have to be vegan to be kind to animals, though taking a moral stand of not causing suffering is extremely laudable. You don't have to be concerned about the world and its survival even though the methane emitted by animals grown for meat is what is causing the world to become warmer and the water to dry up. But you have to be kind to yourself. Just as you would not run your stove on petrol, don't put inappropriate food into your body.

Veganism is not that easy to incorporate into your life. Meat is a drug and once addicted to it, it takes a while to give it up. I would advise that when you are on the road to veganism, stay away from meat-eating environments and people for a while as the smell of cooked meat can bring cravings. There will be a few slips along the way but once your body sheds its addiction and goes forward to good health, there is no turning back.

India is a very exciting place to be vegan. There are so many nutritious but forgotten vegetables and grains in India that need to be reintroduced into our daily diet. Black rice from Meghalaya, pineapples from Manipur, 200 varieties of rajma ranging from white to purple, summer and winter millets, thousands of varieties of leaves, berries and fruits that even I need to learn about....

I am as fierce about the organic food movement as I am about animals and nature. I held the first organic festival in India more than 20 years ago. When I became minister again, I started an annual organic festival in Delhi. Hundreds of women brought produce from all over India. Now these festivals have spread from Delhi to Ahmedabad, Mumbai and Chennai. Customers for organic food have increased every year. I look for women who have regenerated old seeds and old ways of cooking and give them national awards.

I congratulate Mala and Nandini for creating recipes in this book that are easy to cook and are for everyday meals. Vegan and wholesome does not mean exotic or pretentious. It is simply good food with all the bad things kept out - refined and processed ingredients, sugar, oil etc. They have even accommodated the new trend of gluten-free food.

Good food deserves celebration. Good food changes relationships and moods. Good health changes your life and you will never know what it is till you achieve it. This book is a guide. Use it to touch the sky.

Maneka Sanjay Gandhi

Nandini and Mala

FROM THE AUTHORS

WHY WE WROTE THIS BOOK

We wrote our first book - Guilt-free Vegan Cookbook, for the health seekers looking to make healthy and easy multi-cuisine restaurant-style food at home. This way they would not feel the need to go to restaurants and compromise on their healthy food choices.

Soon after we published that book, we started getting requests for more recipes for wholesome, everyday Indian food. This sparked the idea of a cookbook for modern urban Indian homes that enjoy an omelette as much as a dosa for breakfast or relish a kheer as much as a chocolate cake for dessert.

We have used ingredients that are easily available in most organic stores and supermarkets across the country. We have also incorporated a lot of local and seasonal vegetables, millets and seasonings. Many options have been given to substitute produce that may be out of season.

CLIMATE CHANGE & FOOD CHOICES

Our food has a huge impact on greenhouse gas emissions. Some estimates put it as high as 51% of total emissions. Clearing land for livestock used for meat and dairy is the leading cause of forest degradation. Using pesticides and artificial fertilizers is one of the leading causes of water contamination, degradation of soil quality and loss of bees and insects that are so critical for biodiversity.

Eating seasonal and local food is encouraged as imported food contributes to 'food miles' or emissions linked to the distance the food has to travel to get to you.

It is no coincidence that the food that is best for the planet is also best for our health. Locally grown, seasonal, organic and plant-based food has the lowest emissions. Broadly speaking, fruit from native trees requires the lowest inputs and resources, be it land, water or fertilizers. Fresh seasonal fruit is also easily digestible and bursting with nutrients. Locally grown millets are less resource-intensive than the popular rice and wheat varieties. Most local millets require no irrigation and are naturally resilient to pests and insects.

As a thumb rule, if you wish to lower your personal carbon emissions, every meal presents an opportunity to do so. Eat more organic, seasonal, local and fresh plant-based food and you will be cutting out nearly 95% of your food emissions.

WHOLE FOOD PLANT-BASED (WFPB) FOR HEALTH

Whole food plant-based is more than a 'diet'- it is a lifestyle of wholesome eating which shuns all animal-based foods like meat, eggs, dairy, honey and all refined food like oil, sugar, refined white rice and flour etc. It focuses instead on fresh fruits, vegetables, beans, legumes, tubers, seeds, nuts and whole grains.

Additionally, we have gone a step further to curate recipes without wheat to help people looking for gluten-free options. Due to the over-commercialization of wheat, the grains available nowadays are hybrid versions with a high percentage of gluten. Many people are reacting to this high level of gluten showing symptoms of bloating, weight gain, digestive issues and allergies. All the recipes in this book are therefore gluten-free.

We have personally experienced many health benefits and have been advocates of the 'whole food plant-based' lifestyle for the past several years.

There are many medical doctors, nutritionists, health coaches and dietitians who recommend this way of eating to prevent and even reverse common lifestyle diseases like diabetes, heart disease, cancer, hormonal issues and auto-immune conditions, among others. To learn more scientific information about this lifestyle, you can see our recommended list of films and books in the Resource section on pg 236.

HOW TO MAKE THE CHANGE

Switching to a whole food plant-based diet overnight can be a daunting proposition for many, so we recommend a slow and steady approach. Don't worry if you can't do everything at once. It's a skill to be learnt.

Start by trying out some of the recipes, which seem easy for you and match your and your family's tastes. You can try 1-2 new recipes per week, depending on the time you have available.

If you enjoy pizzas, you may want to try the gluten-free base of our Fiery Indian Pizza or if you have only had white rice poha in the past, try our version with brown or red rice. If you cannot conceive of fries without frying, you must try our Sweet Potato Country Fries made completely without oil and are oh-so-delicious, even if we say so ourselves!

If snacking or desserts are your weak spots, try our delicious oil- and sugar-free versions. You will find them filling and satisfying.

We recommend you add a big and juicy salad before every meal. The secret to eating healthy is to eat plenty of fruits and vegetables and as much raw or 'sun-cooked' food as possible. In India, we do not give much thought to our salads, lackadaisically cutting up half a cucumber, tomato and some onions as an afterthought to a meal. Here we bring you many new ideas. Use them to create your own family favourites.

HAVE FUN GOING MORE PLANT-BASED

Show up at a dinner party with one of your favourite dishes from the book. Surprise your friends with an oil-, sugar- and dairy-free creation that is tasty too. Host a potluck and don't tell anyone that the food is plant-based or free of all things unhealthy. Just let them enjoy it and if they like it, tell them afterwards.

Cooking for one's own self is a form of essential self-care. You take more interest in it and you know exactly what is going into your food. Have some fun with it!

If you usually rely on the house help to do all the cooking, get into the kitchen and see how much fun it can be to create something tasty and healthy for yourself and the family! If you cook the same old stuff and hear complaints from the family, surprise them with some easy, healthy new recipes.

If you are a man reading this, don't be dependent on the women to cook your food. Take some initiative in the kitchen too! It's also fun to cook with the kids and create something healthy and nourishing. You are bonding together as a family and teaching them a useful life skill at the same time.

THE TIME IS NOW!

They say the best time to go for a healthy diet and lifestyle was yesterday and the second best time is right now!

Today, the same thing can be said for the health of the planet at large too. Plant-based is the future of food. Thousands across the world are switching their ways of eating to more and more plant-based and wholesome food for better health, climate change considerations and most importantly, compassion towards animals.

Begin today!

WHOLE FOOD PLANT-BASED ESSENTIALS

Whole grains

We replace white flour with whole grain flour and white rice with brown, red or black rice which is rich in fibre, natural fats and nutrients.

Dairy alternatives

A variety of nuts, seeds, legumes etc. are used to replace dairy products.

Dietary fats

All the nuts and seeds from which oil is extracted are used in their wholesome form to provide flavour and essential fats.

Cooking without oil

a. Use heavy-bottomed vessels to avoid sticking and burning of food.

b. For tempering spices, simply roast them on medium heat. Turn off the heat before adding powdered spices, else they will burn. Roasting spices produces distinct aromas signalling that the spice is properly cooked.

c. To sauté without oil, you can add some salt to release water 10 mins before cooking or sprinkle a little water. This prevents sticking to the vessel and burning.

Sugar and sweeteners

We use dried fruit in its whole form and in limited quantities. The fibre present limits the insulin spike in the blood compared to other refined sweeteners.

Gluten-free choices

Avoiding gluten is not necessary under a whole food plant-based plan. However, due to excessive gluten in today's hybrid wheat varieties, many people are developing gluten allergies, so we decided to keep this book gluten-free also.

In India, we are blessed to have dozens of varieties of millets. We have used some of the commonly available millets to substitute wheat which is the primary source of gluten. We have used oats which can be contaminated with gluten, so if you are a celiac or have a severe gluten allergy, please use certified gluten-free oats only.

Avoid peeling

We recommend not peeling the fruits and vegetables that require a peeler except for removing dirty or damaged parts. The peels of most fresh produce offer a variety of nutrients and fibre. The very best nutrition is often right under the peel.

UTENSILS AND ACCESSORIES

Steamer - Stainless steel vessels are usually the best and last long. For efficient cooking of vegetables, you can cook a grain in the bottom level with the water and steam-cook the vegetables on top.

Blender/ Mixer/ Grinder - A good and hardy, local, all-in-one brand with sturdy steel jars for mixer and grinder and clear glass jar for the blender function would be ideal.

Heavy-bottomed woks and pans - For oil-free dosas, chillas and pancakes where the batter is spread on a skillet, please use a very heavy-bottomed stoneware or metal frying pan with a tight fitting lid. This ensures that the food is steamed in its own moisture and the food leaves the bottom of the vessel easily.

Pressure cooker - For cooking hard food items like beans and pulses or whole daals, this is used in all Indian homes. Please use a stainless steel cooker as aluminium has been linked to adverse health effects. Where feasible, we have given the number of whistles and time taken to cook. Timings can vary depending on the level of heat and equipment. Please adjust accordingly.

Oven/ OTG/ Air fryer - We have used a regular convection oven for the baked recipes. You are welcome to use OTG or Air Fryer as per the time and temperature conversions applicable on your appliances.

Silicone sheets or parchment paper - These are essential for baking without oil. They protect the food from sticking to the tray. Buy good quality reusable silicone sheets since they last for years. Parchment paper is also a good alternative.

KITCHEN SUBSTITUTIONS CHART

FOOD/INGREDIENT	Substitution Options
BUTTER	Coconut, avocado, almond butter, cashew butter, peanut butter, pumpkin seed butter, sunflower seed butter, sesame seed butter etc.
BUTTERMILK	Buttermilk made from plant-based curd or from fresh coconut milk.
CHEESE	Cheese made from plant-based sources such as nuts, seeds, and seasoned with nutritional yeast flakes.
CHOCOLATE	Cacao powder, carob powder or vegan dark chocolate.
CREAM	Cashew or coconut cream.
CURD	Curd made from plant-based milks such as soy, peanut, rice etc.
EGGS	Ground flaxseeds whisked with water, soaked chia seeds, or mashed ripe bananas depending on recipe.
FRIED FOOD	Oil-free, baked or roasted alternatives.
GHEE	Dehydrated coconut, ground to ghee-like consistency or cashew butter.
ICE CREAM	Plant-based milk or fruit ice cream sweetened with dried fruit.
MAYONNAISE	Oil-free cashew mayonnaise.
MEAT AND SEAFOOD	Soy nuggets and flakes, tofu, beans, readymade meat replacers, and unripe jackfruit.

FOOD/INGREDIENT	Substitution Options
MILK	Plant-based milk including almond, coconut, cashew, oat, rice, sesame, soy, melon seeds etc.
OIL	Whole nuts, seeds and legumes from which oil is extracted such as coconut, peanuts, sesame seeds, sunflower seeds.
PANEER	Tofu or 'soy paneer' and tofu marinated in cashew cream.
SALAD DRESSING	Oil-free salad dressings and chutneys.
SALT (IODIZED)	Himalayan, rock, or sea salt.
SOFT DRINKS	Water, lime juice with water, coconut water, fruit smoothies, etc.
SUGAR, HONEY, AND ARTIFICIAL SWEETENERS	Dried fruits such as dates, raisins, dried figs and apricots or dry date powder *(kharek)*.
TEA AND COFFEE	Homemade infusions of herbs and spices, readymade herbal teas, and roasted barley or dried peas coffee.
WHITE FLOUR	Whole grains and flour from millets like sorghum, pearl millet, amaranth, buckwheat, finger millet, kodo millet, little millet etc.
WHITE RICE	Whole (unpolished) rice such as brown, red or black rice.

BREAKFAST

Desi Omelette
with Dill and Tomatoes

Serves 4

Ingredients

- 1 cup chickpea flour *(besan)*
- 2-3 tbsp fresh dill (or fresh coriander), finely chopped
- 1 small onion, finely chopped
- 1 medium tomato, finely chopped
- Black salt *(kala namak)*, to taste
- Black pepper, to taste (optional)
- 1 fresh green chilli, finely chopped or ¼ tsp red chilli powder (optional)

Method

1. In a bowl, add the *besan*, salt, pepper and chilli powder (if using). Add 1½ cups of water, pouring it in slowly and whisking continuously to prevent lumps. Once smooth, mix in the chopped dill.
2. In a heavy-bottomed frying pan, dry sauté the onions until slightly brown on medium heat. Sprinkle water if needed, to prevent it from sticking to the pan.
3. Add in the tomatoes and chopped green chillies (if using) and cook for 4-5 minutes until tomatoes are soft. Remove from pan and set aside.
4. Adjust consistency of the *besan* mix as required (like a dosa or waffle batter). Pour into the pan and spread with the back of a spoon making concentric circles from the centre outwards. Now sprinkle the cooked onions and tomatoes evenly across your omelette and cover tightly and cook on medium heat for 4-5 minutes until the bottom begins to brown.
5. Fold over and serve with steamed masala bread toast (pg 165).

Chef's Note: *Kala namak is the essential ingredient of this recipe. It contains sulphur and gives the 'egg-like' smell and taste.*

Scrambled Tofu Bhurji

Serves 4

Ingredients

- 2 cups medium firm tofu, crumbled
- ½ cup onion, chopped
- ½ cup tomato, chopped
- ½ cup fresh coriander, chopped
- ¼ cup spring onion greens, chopped
- ½ tsp green chilli, chopped
- Salt and pepper to taste

Method

1. Sauté the onions and tomatoes in a pan until soft.
2. Add the crumbled tofu and cook it till the water from the tofu dries up.
3. Add coriander, spring onion, green chilli, salt and pepper to taste. Stir until well mixed.
4. Serve hot with toast or *roti* with a sprinkling of fresh coriander.

Jewelled Wholesome Idlis

Serves 4-6

Ingredients

- 2 cups unpolished brown (or red) rice
- ½ cup black gram lentils *(sabut urad daal)*
- 1 tsp fenugreek seeds
- Salt to taste
- ¼ cup french beans, chopped
- ¼ cup carrots, chopped
- ¼ cup corn kernels
- 10-12 curry leaves *(kadi patta)*
- 1 tbsp ginger, grated
- 1 tsp green chilli paste

Method

1. Wash and soak the brown rice and the *urad daal* separately for 6-8 hours. Leave at least 1" water above the *daal* as it will swell up. Soak the fenugreek seeds either with the rice or *daal*.
2. Drain the water next and grind the soaked rice with enough water in a grinder (or a stone idli grinder) till you get a coarse batter which can be poured. Remove into a large bowl to set aside. Separately, grind the soaked *urad daal* with a little water till very smooth and mix together with the rice batter.
3. Set aside this batter in a large bowl so it is less than half full as this would double in volume. Keep the bowl in a warm place to ferment overnight or for 8-14 hours depending on the ambient temperature. In Indian summer heat, 8 hours is sufficient, but in cooler climates, it can take longer. When it has risen in the bowl and has a slightly sour, fermented smell, it's ready.
4. Mix together all the vegetables, setting aside ½ cup for decorating the *idlis*. Mix in the remaining vegetables with the batter, salt, ginger and chilli paste and pour into *idli* moulds in an *idli* steamer.
5. Decorate the tops with the vegetables and add a curry leaf.
6. Steam for 20-25 mins until a knife comes out clean from the steamed *idlis*.
7. Serve with *sambhar* (pg 125) and coconut chutney (pg 214).

Chef's Note – *For making dosa, add ½-1 cup more water to the rice and daal batter (without vegetables) to make it thinner for spreading.*

Ingredients

For 4 Dosas

- 1 cup finger millet *(ragi)* flour
- 1 cup coconut, grated
- 1½ cups water
- Pinch of salt

For the Masala Filling

- 2 medium potatoes, steamed and chopped
- 1 onion, sliced lengthways
- 6-8 curry leaves *(kadi patta)*
- ¼ tsp turmeric
- ½ tsp black mustard seeds
- 1 tsp split bengal gram lentil *(chana daal)*
- 2 dried red chillies (whole)
- Salt to taste
- Sesame Fenugreek Chutney (pg 219)

Neer Ragi Masala Dosa

Serves 2

Method

For the Dosa

1. Mix the dosa ingredients in a bowl to make an instant dosa batter.
2. In a heavy-bottmed frying pan with a tight fitting lid, temper the bottom by putting a couple of drops of oil and spreading with half a chopped potato/onion. This same potato piece can be reused without more oil for 10 dosas.
3. Spread a ladleful of dosa mixture on the pan in a circular motion spreading outward until a very thin layer is formed.
4. Allow the batter to cook on low heat and after a few minutes cover the pan with a tight lid so that the upper part of the dosa also cooks in its own steam.
5. Be careful when you lift off the cover so as to not allow the water droplets to fall on the dosa. Once cooked, the sides will automatically lift up from the surface.
6. Gently scrape the dosa off the pan onto a serving plate.

For the Masala Filling

1. Sprinkle a little salt on the onions and keep aside for 5 minutes to release water so they don't stick while cooking.
2. Meanwhile, roast the *chana daal*, mustard seeds, red chillies and curry leaves in a pan until an aroma is released.
3. Add the onions and turmeric powder and sauté until onions are soft. If required, sprinkle some water to keep them moist without burning.
4. Once the onions are half cooked, add the chopped potatoes and remaining salt and sauté till the mixture is nicely mushy but not completely mashed.
5. Since we are not using any oil, feel free to sprinkle water on it anytime you feel the potato is getting too dry. Try not to mash the potatoes but leave them a little chunky.
6. On each dosa, spread the potatoes on half the dosa and fold the other half over. Sprinkle with sesame fenugreek chutney for an extra punch.
7. Serve with coconut *chutney* (Pg 214) and *sambhar* (Pg 125).

Rustic Poha with Veggies

Serves 4

Ingredients

- 2 cups flattened brown (or red) rice *poha*
- ½ cup onions, thinly sliced
- ½ cup carrots, diced
- ½ cup beans, diced
- ¼ cup peas, shelled
- 1 tsp lemon juice
- 6-8 curry leaves *(kadi patta)*
- ½ tsp black mustard seeds
- 1 tbsp split bengal gram lentil *(chana daal)*
- 2 red dry chillies
- ¼ cup peanuts, roughly chopped
- Salt to taste

Method

1. Sauté the onions in a wok for 2-3 minutes on medium heat. Sprinkle water to avoid burning and sticking to pan. Add all the vegetables and stir for 1-2 minutes. Cover and cook to allow them to steam and soften for 1-2 minutes.
2. Put the poha in a sieve and wash it under running water and drain.
3. Add the washed poha to the vegetables and continue to toss the mixture.
4. Separately roast the tempering ingredients in a small pan adding them in the following order and stirring each for 10-20 seconds till roasted - *chana daal*, black mustard seeds, red chillies and curry leaves. When roasted, add to the poha.
5. Mix the tempering and poha and switch off the heat. Now stir in the lemon juice, salt to taste and peanuts. Serve hot.

Savoury Oats Upma

Serves 2

Ingredients

- 1 cup whole rolled oats
- 2 cups water
- 1 cup mixed vegetables (carrots, beans, peas, onion), diced
- 2 tbsp roasted peanuts, roughly crushed
- 1 tsp lemon juice
- 4-5 curry leaves *(kadi patta)*
- ½ tsp black mustard seeds
- 2 dry red chillies
- Salt to taste

Method

1. In a heavy-bottomed wok or pan, roast the curry leaves, mustard seeds and chillies, stirring them often to prevent burning until the mustard seeds start to pop.
2. Add the vegetables and salt and sprinkle 1-2 tbsp water to prevent it from sticking to the pan.
3. Cover with a lid to allow the vegetables to cook in their own steam.
4. When semi-cooked or al denté, (do not let the vegetables go too soft), add the oats and water and allow to cook for 2-3 minutes. Cook longer if you prefer it softer.
5. Switch off the heat and add the lemon juice and half the peanuts.
6. For serving, pack the upma in small cups and turn them upside down in the serving dishes and garnish with the remaining peanuts.

Crunchy Moong Chilla Rolls

Serves 4

Ingredients

For the Chilla

- 2 cups split yellow lentil *(dhuli moong daal)*, soaked overnight
- ½ cup coriander, chopped
- 1 tbsp green chillies, chopped
- Water as required
- Salt to taste

For Stuffing

- 1 cucumber, julienned
- 2 tomatoes, julienned
- 1 carrot, julienned
- 1 green chilli, finely chopped
- 2 tbsp lime juice
- Salt to taste
- Coconut Chutney (pg 214)

Method

1. Grind together all chilla ingredients to make a batter of pouring consistency.
2. Spread one ladleful on a flat heavy-bottomed pan or *dosa tawa* in circular motion with the back of a spoon, starting from the centre of the pan. Cover with a tight fitting lid and steam for 2-3 minutes.
3. Allow the chilla to cook until it can be lifted easily from the pan. Turn over to cook the other side. When slightly brown, set chilla aside on a plate.
4. Mix all the julienned vegetables with chopped green chillies, lime juice and salt.
5. To assemble, spread coconut chutney generously on half the chilla and place some vegetables lengthways on top.
6. Roll the chilla tightly and cut into bite size pieces.
7. Serve immediately to maintain crispness.

Red Rice Appam with Ishtew

Appams

Makes 6-8 appams

Ingredients

- 1 cup red rice
- ½ cup fresh coconut, grated
- ½ tbsp yeast
- Salt to taste

Method

1. Wash and soak the red rice for 4-6 hours.
2. Drain the water and transfer to a grinder. Add the grated coconut and 1/2 cup of water and grind to a smooth batter.
3. Pour into a large bowl with plenty of empty space as the batter will double in volume. Stir in the salt and yeast and cover it with a plate and set aside in a warm place for 8-12 hours or overnight.
4. Add more water if necessary to ensure it is pouring consistency like a dosa batter when you make the appams.
5. In Kerala a traditional vessel *(appam kadhai)* is used for making appams. You can also use a flat griddle. Using a ladle, scoop some batter into the *kadhai* and spread by circling the pan while holding it up with the handles. If using a griddle, spread the mixture in a circular motion till the desired size.
6. Keep the centre a little thicker than the edges to get the lace effect. Cover and allow it to cook in its steam for a minute on one side only. Further cook uncovered till the edges become crisp.
7. When slightly brown and the appam leaves the bottom of the pan, it is ready. Using a flat spatula carefully remove the appam from the pan. Serve hot with ishtew.

Ishtew

Serves 4

Ingredients

- 1 cup broken cauliflower florets
- ½ carrot, sliced
- ½ cup peas, shelled
- 8 beans, chopped into 1" pieces
- 4 baby onions, peeled
- 2 medium-sized potatoes, diced (with skin)
- 2 sticks cinnamon
- 1 tbsp ginger, grated
- 4 cloves
- 2 bay leaves
- 4 cardamoms
- ½ tsp black peppercorns
- 2 cups thick coconut milk (pg 225)
- ¼ cup fresh coconut, shredded
- Salt to taste

Method

1. Put all the vegetables and spices into a pan with 1 cup water and bring to a boil. Lower the heat allowing the vegetables to soften slightly and yet remain crunchy.
2. Grind the shredded coconut with 1/2 cup water to yield a paste and add to the vegetables along with the salt and coconut milk.
3. Heat without boiling and serve hot with appams

Lentil Bread Sandwhich

Makes 4

Ingredients

- For the loaf, follow the recipe for the masala bread (pg 165) except leave out all the masala from it.
- 2 tomatoes, sliced
- ½ cucumber, sliced
- I onion, sliced and separated into rings
- 1 tbsp green chutney (pg 214)
- 2 tbsp fresh coriander, chopped
- 1 green chilli, chopped
- 1 tbsp lemon juice
- Salt to taste

Method

1. Slice the loaf into 1 cm thick slices.
2. Spread the green chutney lightly on the slices.
3. Layer in the tomato, cucumber and onion.
4. Sprinkle the chopped coriander and green chilli as per taste.
5. Squeeze some lemon and add salt.
6. Close the sandwich with another slice.

Nutty Amaranth Porridge

Serves 4-6

Ingredients

- ½ cup raw almonds, soaked overnight
- 1 cup amaranth, popped
- 1/2 cup (or as per taste) date paste (pg 232)
- ½ cup walnuts and cashew nuts, roughly broken
- ¼ cup of mixed dried berries - blueberries, black currants, raisins, sultanas, cranberries (use any 2-3 of your choice in equal proportions)
- ½ tsp cinnamon powder

Method

1. Blend the almonds with 1 cup water to make a thick milk. We like keeping the peel of the almonds intact for the fibre. You can add more water to the milk for the desired consistency.
2. If you want to serve this hot, heat the milk to desired temperature (but don't boil) and add all the remaining ingredients. Adjust sweetness by adding more date paste if required.
3. If you want to serve this at room temperature, stir in all the ingredients and allow to sit for 10 minutes for the flavours to merge.

Fit and Fab Granola

Serves 4-6

Ingredients

- 2 cups almond milk (pg 222)

For Granola

- 1 cup rolled oats
- 3 cups mixture of the following ingredients, roughly broken or chopped:
  - ½ cup walnuts
  - ½ cup almonds
  - ½ cup black raisins
  - ½ cup dried apricots
  - ¼ cup cashews
  - ¼ cup green raisins
  - ¼ cup cranberries
  - ¼ cup dried figs
- 2 tbsp date paste (pg 232)
- 1 tsp cinnamon powder

Method

1. Mix well all the dry ingredients and date paste and spread on a baking tray.
2. Bake at 180°C for 10-15 minutes. Turn the mixture every 5 minutes until it becomes evenly crisp.
3. Allow to cool completely as the granola will be crunchier. Enjoy with fresh coconut or almond milk.

Chef's note: *This dry granola will stay fresh in an airtight jar for 3 weeks and a little longer in the fridge.*

Fruity Green Smoothie Bowl

Serves 2

Ingredients

- 2 very ripe bananas, chopped and frozen overnight
- 1 cup packed, tender spinach leaves
- Seasonal fruit assortment for decoration
  Here we have used:
  - ½ peach, sliced
  - ¼ cup pomegranate arils
  - ½ dragon fruit, chopped or made into balls with a melon scooper
  - 1-2 cherries and strawberries for decoration
- 1 tbsp walnuts, roughly chopped
- 1 tbsp black currants
- Few pieces of toasted coconut slices

Method

1. Pull out the bananas from the freezer to thaw for 5-10 minutes till they can be pulled apart.
2. Use ½ cup of water to blend the spinach leaves to a fine paste.
3. Add the frozen bananas and blend to a thick green smoothie.
4. Pour into a bowl and decorate with the assortment of fruit and nuts as shown.

Chef's Note: *You can use any seasonal fruits for the toppings as per local availability. The idea is to make it look colourful and attractive.*

Purple Chia Summer Cooler

Serves 3

Ingredients

- 3 tbsp chia (or *sabja*) seeds, soaked in 1/2 cup water for 1-2 hours
- 1-2 tsp fresh beetroot juice
- 1/2 cup coconut cream (pg 226)
- 1 kiwi, thinly sliced into rounds
- 1 orange, thinly sliced into rounds (keep peel)
- 6 cherries
- ½ cup fresh pomegranate arils
- 1 cup mixed fresh fruit, chopped (mix of apple, kiwi and banana)
- 1 tbsp raisins, chopped into halves

Method

1. Mix the beetroot juice a few drops at a time with the soaked chia seeds to get the right shade of purple you require. You can add a little of the coconut cream to adjust the required colour.
2. Fill the bottom of a tall glass about 1/3 with the purple chia seeds.
3. Making sure the inside of the glass is dry place a row of sliced kiwi around the inside of the glass so it sticks to the sides.
4. Next place a row of sliced orange above the kiwi slices. Mix the chopped fruit and raisins. Fill the glass with this fruit salad without disturbing the kiwi and orange slices and ensure they remain intact on the inside of the glass.
5. Drop some pomegranate arils on top allowing them to fill the gaps along the sides of the fruit salad.
6. Top up the glass with some coconut cream and decorate with cherries, orange and kiwi slices as shown.

Chef's Note: *To save time, you can skip the decoration on the inside of the glass with the thin fruit slices and follow the rest of the recipe.*

Mango and Peach Tango

Serves 2

Ingredients

- 1 cup mangoes, chopped
- 1 cup mangoes, pulped
- 1 cup peaches, chopped
- ½ cup pomegranate arils
- 4 cherries for decoration (optional)

Method

1. In a bowl, mix the chopped mangoes, peaches and pomegranate and scoop a few spoonfuls into the bottom of a clear glass
2. Pour in some mango pulp topped with more mixed fruit. Keep layering till you reach the top.
3. Decorate with a couple of cherries.

Fruit Cream

Serves 2

Ingredients

- 1 cup mixed seasonal fruit, chopped e.g. apple, kiwi, banana, pomegranate
- ½ cup tender coconut thick flesh *(moti malai)*, chopped
- ½ tsp vanilla powder (optional)
- 1 tsp lime juice (optional)
- 1/4 cup raisin paste (pg 233)
- 1 tbsp pistachio flakes for garnish

Method

1. To make the coconut cream, blend the tender coconut with the raisin paste using the soaking water of the raisins. The raisins will give it a sour, yogurt-like taste. If you want it more sour, add the lime juice. Add the vanilla powder, if using. Mix well.

2. In a tall lass, scoop some fruit at the bottom, then a layer of the coconut cream, then another layer of fruit and repeat till you reach the top. Garnish with pistachio flakes.

Chef's Note: *You could use any seasonal fruit like grapes, papapya, peaches, pineapple, strawberries, cherries, mango etc. You can also flavour the cream with freshly chopped mint and garnish with a sprig of mint.*

SALADS

Rainbow Rolls

Makes 6 Rolls

Ingredients

For the Salad

- 1 medium head of green cabbage
- ¼ red cabbage, sliced finely lengthways
- 1 red capsicum, sliced lengthways
- 1 yellow capsicum, sliced lengthways
- 1 cucumber (or zucchini), sliced into sticks
- 1 carrot, coarsely grated

For the Dip

- 2 tbsp peanut butter (Pg 228)
- 2 tbsp tamarind paste (Pg 234)
- 1 soft date, pitted
- Pinch of asafoetida *(heeng)*
- Salt to taste

Method

1. Cut off the base stem of the cabbage and carefully remove 6 leaves so as not to tear them.
2. Blanch the leaves in boiling hot water for 1-2 minutes to soften them enough to roll without cracking.
3. Layout the cabbage leaf and pile in the vegetables, roll tightly and pierce with a toothpick to hold in place.
4. To make the dip, blend all the ingredients together with as little water as required to move the blades and make a thick dipping sauce.

Chef's Note: *You can substitute peanut butter with sunflower seed butter, sesame butter or almond butter.*

Cheesy Cherry Tomato Salad

Serves 4

Ingredients

For the Salad

- 2 cups cherry tomatoes, halved
- ½ cup basil leaves, packed tight
- ½ cup parsley, chopped
- ½ lime, thinly sliced

For the Cheese

- 1 cup hard tofu, crumbled
- 2 tbsp lime juice
- 1 tsp roasted cumin, crushed or powdered
- Salt and pepper to taste
- Red chilli powder to taste

Method

1. Mix all the cheese ingredients and marinate for 30 minutes to 1 hour.
2. Mix in with all the salad ingredients before serving.

Chef's Note: *You can substitute parsley with coriander.*

Beetroot Parcels with Avocado

Serves 4

Ingredients

- 2 large size beetroots
- 2 tbsp savoury cashew cream for garnish (optional) (Pg 229)

For the Guacamole Dip

- 1 avocado, mashed with a fork
- ½ onion, finely chopped
- 1 tomato, finely chopped
- 1 green chilli, minced (optional)
- 1 tsp lemon juice
- Salt to taste

Method

1. Slice the beetroots into thin and large slices for rolling. Do not use the side slices as they will be too small.
2. Blanch the slices in hot, salted water to soften them.
3. Mix all the guacamole dip ingredients together.
4. Top each slice with a teaspoon of guacamole dip and roll. Secure with a toothpick if necessary.
5. Pile the rolls up into a pyramid and pour a teaspoon of cashew cream for garnishing on each (if using).

Beetroot Kosambri

Serves 4

Ingredients

For the Salad

- 1 small beetroot, sliced lengthways
- ½ carrot, julienned
- ½ cucumber, julienned
- ½ raw mango, julienned (optional)
- 1 green chilli, chopped
- ¼ tsp black pepper, freshly ground
- ½ cup dehusked black gram lentil *(dhuli urad daal)*, soaked overnight
- 1 tbsp lemon juice (omit if using raw mango)
- Salt to taste

For the Tempering

- ½ tsp mustard seeds
- Pinch of asafoetida *(heeng)*
- 8-10 curry leaves *(kadi patta)*

Method

1. Combine all the salad ingredients in a bowl and mix well.
2. In a pan, roast the mustard seeds and curry leaves till the seeds pop. Turn off heat and roast the asafoetida (to prevent burning).
3. Add the tempering over the vegetable mixture. Adjust the salt and serve.

Cucumber Boats

Serves 4

Ingredients

- 2 cucumbers, sliced half, lengthways
- 1 cup corn kernels
- ½ cup coconut, finely grated
- ¼ cup green coriander, chopped
- 1" ginger
- 1 tbsp raisin paste (pg 233)
- ½ tsp green chillies, chopped (optional)
- 1 tbsp lime juice
- Salt to taste

Method

1. Lightly steam the corn kernels over boiling water for 2-3 minutes till soft enough to eat yet bright in colour and not mushy. Allow to cool.
2. Scrape out the seeds from the cucumber to form a hollow 'boat'.
3. Grind together the ginger, raisin paste, lime juice, salt and green chillies (if using), to a thick and smooth paste.
4. Mix all the ingredients except cucumbers, together with the cooled peas and corn.
5. Stuff this mixture into the cucumber boats and serve.

Chef's note: *For a raw version of the dish, use tender corn.*

Spinach Paan

Serves 4

Ingredients

For the Salad

- 8-12 large leaves of spinach, washed and pat dried
- 1 cup dried coconut flakes
- ½ cup peanuts, roasted and coarsely broken
- 2 limes, pits removed and diced with skin
- 1 inch ginger, minced

For the Dressing

- ¼ cup raisin paste (Pg 233)
- 1 tbsp ginger, grated
- 4-6 tbsp soy sauce

Method

1. Grind together all the dressing ingredients to form a smooth and thick sauce. Add the soaking raisin water if necessary to move the blades.
2. Lay out the leaves of spinach on a flat surface. Heap them with 2 tbsp coconut flakes each.
3. Distribute the remaining ingredients equally among the leaves or as per taste.
4. Fold and enjoy like a paan. You can pierce the paan with a toothpick to hold it together.

Fiery Radish Salad

Serves 2

Ingredients

- 1 white radish *(mooli)*, grated
- 4 tbsp lemon juice
- 2 tbsp fresh coriander leaves
- 1 green chilli, finely chopped
- I tbsp mustard powder
- Salt to taste

Method

1. Mix all the ingredients together and adjust the taste according to your preference.
2. Serve immediately, else the radish will get watery.

Chef's Note – *This is an extra pungent salad which goes well with bland dishes.*

Ingredients

For the Salad

- 1½ cups red (or green) cabbage, julienned
- 1½ cups carrots, julienned
- 1 cup red capsicum, julienned
- 1 cup raw mangoes, julienned
- 1 cup onions, thinly sliced
- 1 cup cashew mayonnaise (Pg 230)
- ¼ tsp black pepper, crushed

For Garnishing

- Few lettuce leaves
- Black peppercorns in brine (optional)

Peppered Indian Coleslaw

Serves 4

Method

1. Mix all the salad ingredients together.
2. Sprinkle a pinch of pepper on top and garnish with lettuce and whole peppercorns.
3. Serve fresh arranged in a nice glass as shown.

Kachumber Sprout Salad

Serves 4

Ingredients

- 8-10 lettuce leaves, washed and pat dried
- Mixed sprouts (*moong,* black gram, chickpeas etc.)
- 1 cup potato, steamed, unpeeled and diced
- 1 cup tomato, diced
- 1 red or green chilli, sliced
- 1 tbsp coriander or parsley, chopped
- ½ cup onion, diced
- ½ cup carrot, shredded
- 1 tbsp roasted watermelon/ sunflower seeds or peanuts to add crunch
- 2 tbsp lime juice
- Salt to taste

Method

1. Lay out the lettuce leaves on a tray.
2. Mix all the remaining ingredients together.
3. Scoop onto the lettuce leaves before serving.

Cucumber Coconut Salad

Serves 4

Ingredients

- 2 cucumbers, unpeeled and diced
- ½ cup roasted peanuts, roughly crushed
- 1 tbsp lime juice
- ¼ cup fresh coriander, chopped
- 1 tbsp raisin paste (Pg 233)
- 1tsp green chillies, minced (optional)
- 2 tbsp mature coconut, grated
- Salt to taste

Method

1. Mix together all the ingredients. Garnish with some coriander and coconut.

Apple Carrot Beet Salad

Serves 2

Ingredients

- 1 apple, julienned
- 1carrot, julienned
- I beetroot, julienned
- 1 tbsp lemon juice
- Salt to taste

Method

1. Mix the apple with the lime juice and set aside to prevent discolouring.
2. Toss together all the ingredients only when ready to serve or the beetroot will bleed into the other vegetables too early.
3. Just before serving, add the salt and toss again.

Chef's Note: *Although it is not recommended to mix fruits and vegetables together due to different digestion times, we use it occasionally for a sweet touch in the salad.*

Tangy Mango Salad

Serves 2

Ingredients

- 1 ripe mango, julienned
- ½ cup cherry tomatoes, halved
- 2 tbsp lemon juice
- 3-4 sticks green beans, finely julienned
- ¼ tsp red chilli flakes (optional)
- 1 tsp white sesame seeds
- Salt to taste

Method

1. Toss together all the ingredients and adjust the seasoning according to taste.
2. Serve fresh.

Chef's Note: *Although it is not recommended to mix fruits and vegetables together due to different digestion times, we use it occasionally for a sweet touch in the salad.*

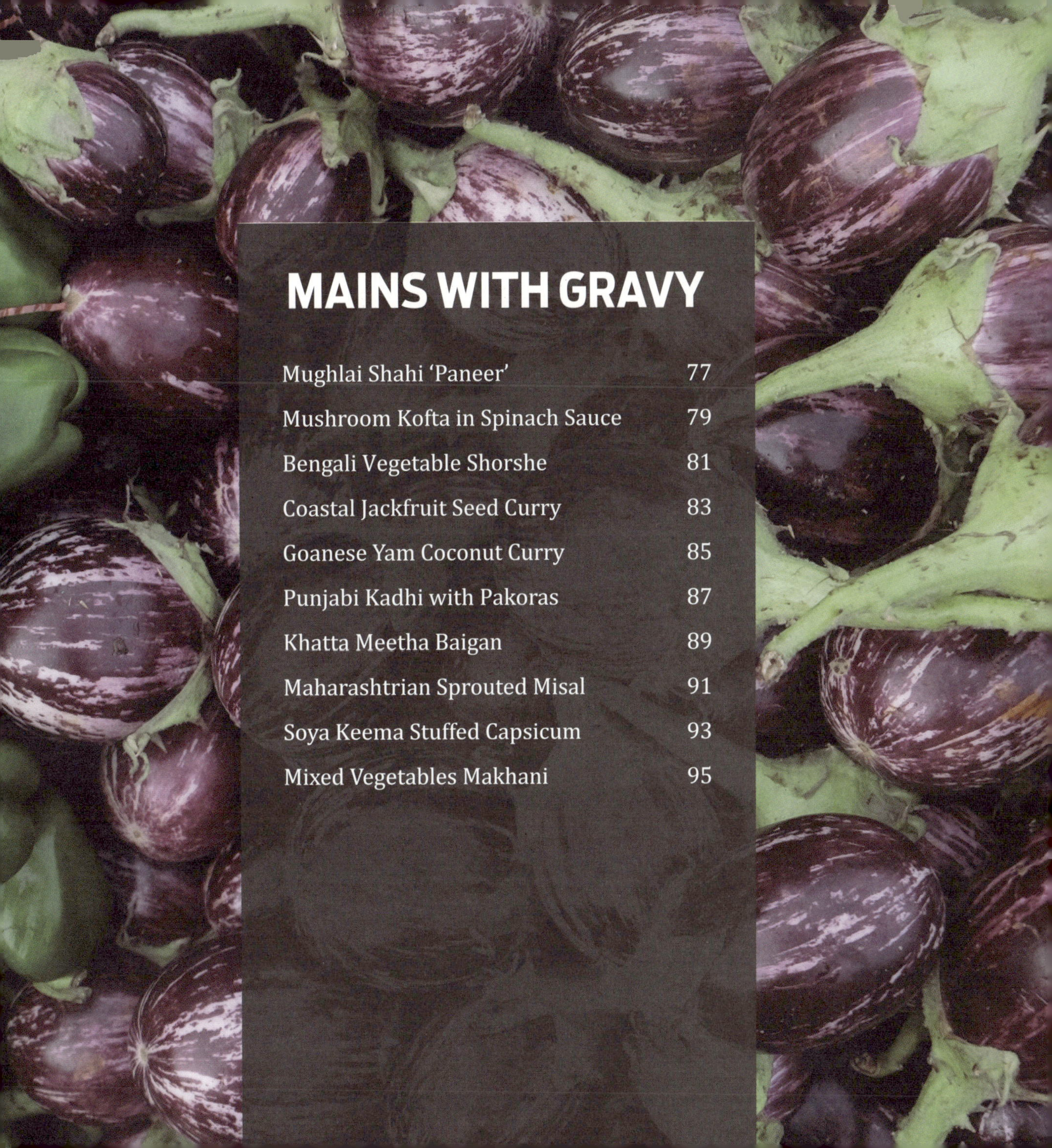

MAINS WITH GRAVY

Mughlai Shahi 'Paneer'

Serves 4

Ingredients

- 2 cups hard tofu, water squeezed out and 1"cubed
- 2 large tomatoes, roughly chopped and blended
- 1 onion, grated
- 1 tsp ginger paste
- 1 tsp garlic paste
- 1 tsp chilli powder
- 2 cinnamon sticks, 1" each
- 2 bay leaves
- 2 black cardamoms
- 2 green cardamoms
- 2 cloves
- ½ cup cashews, soaked for 2-3 hours
- Salt to taste

Method

1. Discard the soaking water of the cashews and blend them with ¼ cup of fresh water and salt to make a smooth and creamy paste.
2. Marinate the tofu cubes in the cashew paste for 30 minutes.
3. In a wok, roast the cinnamon, cardamoms, cloves and bay leaves until the fragrance is released.
4. Add the ginger, garlic and onion and cook for 4-5 minutes on medium heat until browned, stirring it continuously. Sprinkle a little water if needed, to avoid it from sticking to the pan.
5. Add the blended tomato, chilli powder and salt and continue cooking on low heat for 7-8 minutes till you get an aroma.
6. Add the marinated tofu along with the cashew paste to the tomato curry, and cook for 5 minutes on medium heat.
7. Adjust thickness of the gravy with more water according to required consistency. If served with rice it can be more runny and if served with *rotis* it can be thicker. Serve hot.

Mushroom Kofta in Spinach Sauce

Serves 4

Ingredients

For the Mushroom Balls

- 2 cups button mushrooms, chopped
- 1 cup walnuts
- 2 tbsp oats
- 1 cup packed coriander or parsley
- ¼ tsp *garam masala*
- Salt to taste

For the Spinach Sauce

- 500 g spinach
- 2 onions, roughly chopped
- ½ tbsp garlic paste
- ½ tbsp ginger paste
- 1 tsp coriander powder
- 1 tsp cumin powder
- ¼ tsp chilli powder
- 1 medium tomato, blended
- 2 black cardamom
- 2 sticks cinnamon 1" each
- 2 bay leaves

Method

1. Add ½ tsp salt to the onion to allow it to release its own water for 10 minutes.
2. Blanch the spinach in boiling water till just wilted and set aside to cool.
3. In a food processor, add all the mushroom ball ingredients and process coarsely. Remove and shape into balls. You can use these raw or as an option, you can bake the mushroom balls at 200oC for 20 minutes, turning them midway for even baking.
4. In a wok, sauté the chopped onions, ginger and garlic paste on medium heat till brown.
5. Add cumin, coriander, chilli powder, tomato paste, cinnamon, cardamom, bay leaves and salt. Cook thoroughly until an aroma is released.
6. Purée the spinach leaves in a wet grinder and add it to the wok. Add some water if necessary so it is not too dry. Let it cook for 4-5 minutes on medium heat until it just begins to boil.
7. Add mushroom balls to the spinach curry. Mix carefully so as not to break the balls and turn off the heat and cover and let it sit for 5 minutes. Serve hot.

Bengali Vegetable Shorshe

Serves 4

Ingredients

- 2 cups of 4-5 mixed vegetables (choose any from beans, carrots, cauliflower, peas, bottle gourd or pumpkin), chopped in 1-2" pieces
- 1 onion, grated
- 2 cloves garlic, grated
- ½ tsp turmeric
- 4 tbsp black mustard seeds, ground
- 1 large tomato, chopped
- 2 green chillies
- Salt to taste

Method

1. Steam cook the vegetables for 3-5 minutes, retaining the crunch.
2. In a grinder add one chilli, salt, turmeric, mustard powder, ½ cup water and grind to a smooth paste. Add in another ½ cup of water and pulse to mix. Set aside.
3. In a wok, sauté the grated onion and garlic till brown. Sprinkle water to prevent it from sticking to the pan.
4. Add the steamed vegetables and tomato paste and mix thoroughly. You can chop and add in the remaining green chilli if needed.
6. Cook the vegetables in this sauce for 5 minutes until gravy thickens and the vegetables are well covered in the sauce. Serve hot with rice.

Coastal Jackfruit Seed Curry

Serves 4

Ingredients

- 2 cups ripe jackfruit seeds
- 2 large tomatoes, blended to a paste
- 2 large onions, blended to a paste
- ½ tbsp ginger paste
- 1 tbsp garlic paste
- ½ tsp *garam masala* powder
- 2 cups medium-thick coconut milk (pg 225)
- Salt to taste

For the Tempering

- ½ tsp mustard seeds
- 10 curry leaves *(kadi patta)*
- 2 dried red chillies

Method

1. Boil the jackfruit seeds with 1 tsp salt in 3 cups of water for 10-12 minutes till soft. Peel seeds after cooling.
2. Sauté the grated onions, garlic and ginger together until slightly brown. Sprinkle water when necessary to prevent it from sticking to the pan.
3. Add the tomatoes, *garam masala* and salt and cook covered on medium heat for about 10 minutes until the entire *masala* is cooked and all raw spice aromas is gone.
4. Add the jackfruit seeds and stir and cook covered for another 2-3 minutes. Add the coconut milk and heat through to the desired temperature. Switch off the heat.
5. Sauté the tempering ingredients in a pan on a medium flame until the seeds pop and the aroma is released. Pour over the curry. Serve hot with rice or millets.

Goanese Yam Coconut Curry

Serves 4

Ingredients

- 1½ cups yam, cut into 2-3" cubes
- 1 red pepper, sliced lengthways into 6-8 slices
- 3 cups medium- thick coconut milk (pg 225)
- 1 medium onion, finely chopped
- Salt to taste

For the Goa Masala

- 1" piece ginger
- 4 cloves garlic
- 2 tsp kashmiri chilli or paprika powder
- ½ tsp cumin seeds or powder
- 3 cloves
- ¼ tsp cinnamon powder
- 6-8 black peppercorns
- ¼ cup balsamic or apple cider vinegar

Method

1. Pressure cook the yam pieces with salt and 2 cups of water for 10 minutes or 2 whistles until soft and a fork can pierce them easily. Allow the yam to cool slightly and pierce with a fork on all sides to allow the masala to be absorbed.
2. While the yam is being prepared, grind together all the masala ingredients into a fine paste. This paste can stay for 3 months, so if you like you can make a large batch and store in the fridge.
3. In a pan on medium flame, add 1 cup of water, the masala and the onion and stir and cook until the water is almost gone and you are left with a thick paste.
4. Add the cooked yam pieces, 1 cup of water and salt and stir thoroughly to mix and bring to a boil.
5. Once boiling, lower the heat, add the red pepper slices and coconut milk. Heat to the temperature preferred for eating and switch off the heat and let it rest covered till it is time to serve. We like the red peppers to be a bit crunchy and juicy. Serve hot with rice or millets.

Punjabi Kadhi With Pakoras

Serves 4

Ingredients

For the Fritters *(Pakoras)*
- 4 tbsp heaped chickpea flour *(besan)*
- 1 onion, chopped
- 1 green chilli, chopped
- 1 tbsp coriander, chopped
- ¼ tsp baking soda
- Salt to taste

For the Curry Sauce
- 1 cup curd (Pg 224)
- 1 cup water
- 1 tbsp chickpea flour *(besan)*
- ¼ tsp turmeric
- ½ tsp dried mango powder *(amchur)*

For the Tempering
- ¼ tsp black mustard seed
- 8 fresh or dried curry leaves *(kadi patta)*
- 2 dried red chillies
- ¼ tsp chilli powder (optional)

Method

1. To make the fritters, mix all the ingredients together adding a little water at a time for the right consistency to roll into balls with your palms.
2. Bake in the oven at 200° C for 30-35 minutes turning the fritters at half time. They should be slightly browned and crisp. (You can also enjoy just the fritters as a snack with a green chutney).
3. For the curry sauce, roast the *besan* on low heat for 5-7 minutes till it emits an aroma. Cool and blend with the remaining curry sauce ingredients to form a smooth sauce. Slow cook on low heat for 20 minutes stirring periodically. Turn off the heat.
4. Place the fritters gently in the curry sauce and cover and let them soak for about 10 minutes while you prepare the tempering.
5. In a small pan on medium heat, roast the tempering ingredients till a fragrance is released and the mustard seeds begin to pop. Sprinkle over the kadhi and serve hot with rice or millets.

Khatta Meetha Baigan

Serves 4

Ingredients

- 8 small size eggplants
- 1 big onion, finely chopped
- 1 big tomato, finely chopped
- 2 tbsp tamarind paste (pg 234)
- 4 tbsp date paste (pg 232)
- ½ tsp black mustard seeds
- ½ tsp chilli powder
- ½ tsp turmeric
- A pinch of asafoetida *(heeng)*
- ½ cup curry leaves *(kadi patta)*
- Salt to taste

Method

1. Halve the eggplants length-ways and marinate in the turmeric and salt for ½ an hour to release the water from them.
2. Cook the eggplants in a covered pan on medium heat until they are brown and soft enough to eat. Set aside.
3. Sauté the curry leaves, mustards seeds and asafoetida till an aroma is released.
4. Add the onion, tomato, chilli powder and salt. Sprinkle water periodically and cook till the mixture is soft and forms a paste.
5. Add tamarind paste, date paste and ½ cup water and simmer for 2-3 minutes.
6. Add the eggplants and mix well. Do not cook further or the eggplant will disintegrate. Serve hot.

Maharashtrian Sprouted Misal

Serves 4

Ingredients

- 2 cups mixed mung beans *(sabut moong)* and black chickpea *(kala chana)* sprouts
- 2 onions, finely chopped
- 4 tomatoes, finely chopped
- 4 cloves of garlic, finely chopped
- 1" ginger, finely chopped
- ¼ tsp turmeric
- ¼ tsp coriander powder
- Salt to taste

For Garnish

- ½ cup onion, finely chopped
- 2 tbsp fresh coriander leaves, chopped (optional)
- 1 green chilli, chopped
- 1-2 tbsp lime juice

Method

1. Sauté the onion, ginger and garlic in a pan till golden brown. Sprinkle water if needed to avoid it from sticking to the pan.
2. Add the tomatoes and cover the pan. Allow the tomatoes to simmer for 7 to 10 minutes until it forms a purée.
3. Add the sprouts, turmeric, coriander powder and salt to the cooked puree and cover the pan.
4. Cook for another 7 minutes, stirring it from time to time.
5. When cooked, sprinkle the fresh coriander leaves (if using), raw onion, green chilli and a dash of lime juice & serve hot.

Soya Keema Stuffed Capsicum

Serves 4

Ingredients

- 2 green capsicums

For the Filling

- 1 cup soya nuggets, soaked for an hour
- 1 onion, finely chopped
- 1 tomato, finely chopped
- ½ tsp cumin powder
- ½ tsp coriander powder
- ½ tsp garlic paste
- ½ tsp ginger paste
- ½ fresh green chilli, chopped
- 1 tbsp fresh coriander leaves
- Salt to taste

For the Sauce

- 4 tomatoes, blended
- 1 onion, grated
- 2 cloves garlic, grated
- 1" ginger, grated
- Salt to taste

Method

1. Sauté the onion, tomatoes, garlic, ginger, cumin powder and coriander powder together until aroma is released. Sprinkle water if the masala sticks to the pan and allow the masala to brown.
2. Drain the water from the soaked nuggets and stir them into the masala. Cook for about 5 minutes until the water has evaporated. Add the fresh green chilli and salt.
3. Meanwhile, cut the caps off the green peppers and scoop the insides clean with a spoon. Stuff the soya nugget mixture into the peppers and set aside.
4. For the sauce, sauté the onion, garlic and ginger till golden brown. Sprinkle water if required, to keep the paste moist and not sticking to the pan. Add the tomato paste and salt. Stir for about 5 minutes until the sauce is cooked.
5. Place the stuffed peppers on the sauce and cover and simmer for 5 minutes. Turn the peppers around carefully to cook on the underside and when the whole of the pepper is semi soft turn off the heat. Serve hot with rice or millets.

Mixed Vegetables Makhani

Serves 4

Ingredients

- 6-8 tomatoes
- ½ cup pumpkin, cubed
- ½ cup cotatoearrots, cubed
- 1 cup ps, cubed
- ½ cup beans, chopped
- ½ cup cauliflower, cut into small florets
- 1/4 cup corn kernels
- 1 tbsp dried fenugreek leaves *(kasuri methi)*
- 1 tsp cumin seeds
- 1 green chilli, sliced (optional)
- Salt to taste
- 2 tbsp coriander, chopped
- ½ cup plain cashew cream (Pg 229)

Method

1. Steam cook the tomatoes for approximately 10 minutes till the skin splits. Allow to cool and grind to a smooth paste with the peel.
2. Steam cook the vegetables for 5-7 minutes leaving them firm and crunchy.
3. In a wok on medium heat, add the cumin, fenugreek leaves and green chilli and roast till they release an aroma.
4. Add the tomato paste and salt and bring to a boil. Add the steamed vegetables and cook for 3-5 minutes.
5. Turn off the heat and add the cashew cream, mixing thoroughly.
6. Garnish with chopped coriander before serving.

Chef's Note: *You can also use any seasonal vegetables like mushrooms, peas, broccoli, zucchini etc.*

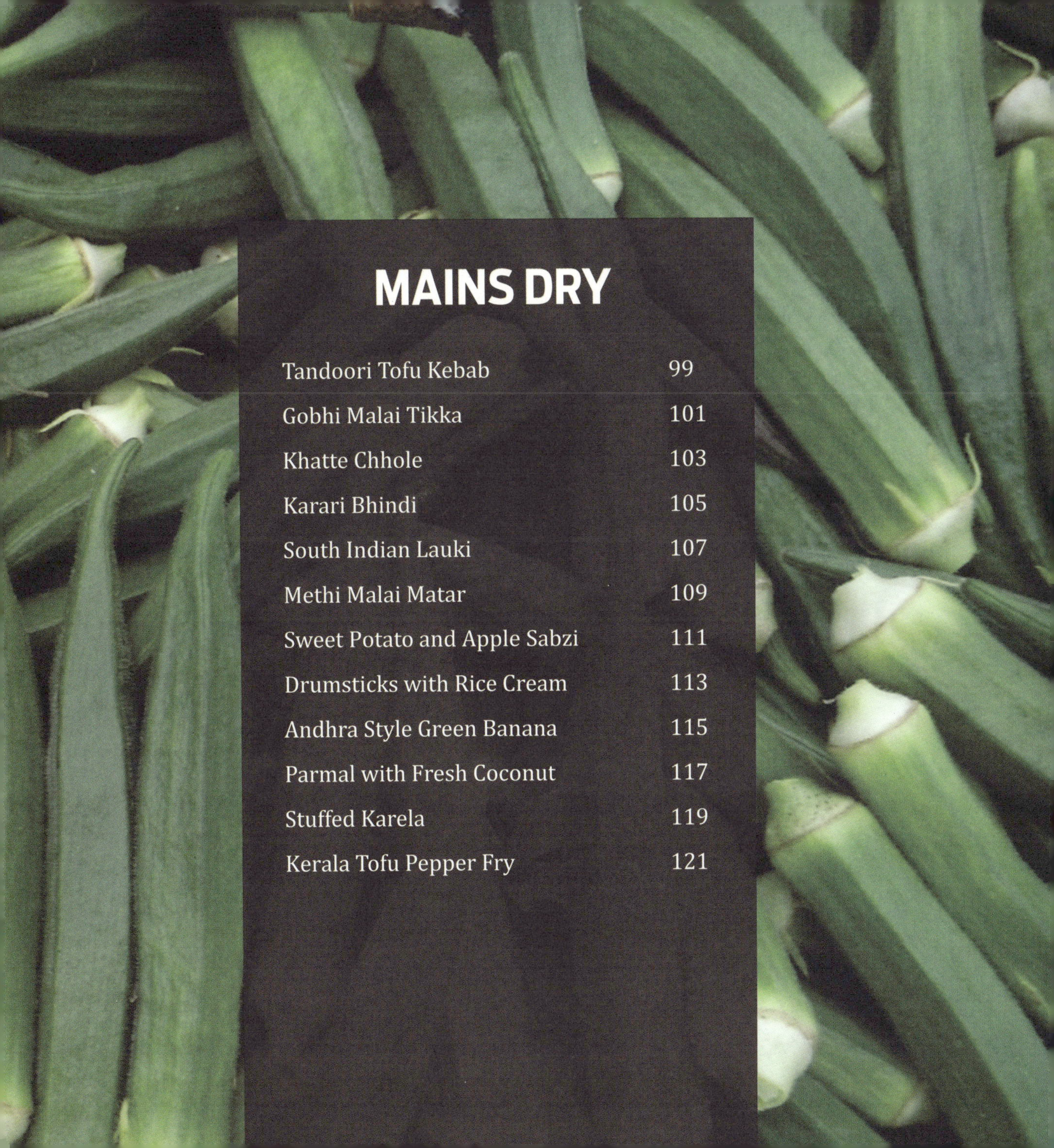

MAINS DRY

Tandoori Tofu Kebab

Serves 4

Ingredients

- 8 pieces firm tofu, 1"-2" cubed
- ½ tsp ginger paste
- ½ tsp garlic paste
- 2 tbsp lemon juice
- 1 big tomato, 1"-2" cubed
- 1 green pepper, cut in 1"-2" squares
- 1 onion, cut in 1"-2" squares
- ½ tsp black pepper powder
- Black salt *(kala namak)* to taste
- 4 skewers

Method

1. Mix all the ingredients together and allow to marinate for 2 hours.
2. Arrange on skewers for grilling as shown.
3. Grill on high heat until golden brown turning the skewers around as they cook and keep basting them with the juice that drips off at every turn. This would take 7-10 minutes depending on the grill size and heat.
4. Remove from heat when done and sprinkle more lemon juice and black salt if required. Serve hot with Green Chutney (pg 214).

Gobhi Malai Tikka

Serves 4

Ingredients

- 1 cauliflower *(gobhi)*

For the Marinade

- 4 tbsp plain cashew cream (pg 229)
- 2 tsp lemon juice
- 1 tsp ginger paste
- 1 tsp garlic paste
- ½ tsp red chilli powder
- ½ tsp cumin powder
- 1 tsp coriander powder
- ¼ tsp turmeric
- Salt to taste

For Garnishing

- 1 onion, sliced and separated into rings
- Black salt
- Pinch of chilli powder

Method

1. Cut the cauliflower into 2" or bite-sized florets.
2. Mix the marinade ingredients in a bowl and add the cauliflower to marinate for approximately 3-4 hours.
3. Now spread the florets on a wide pan and sprinkle the black salt and onion rings on them.
4. Heat the grill (or use a *tandoor*/barbecue) to cook the cauliflower on medium-high heat for 10-15 minutes and then on high heat for 2-3 minutes to brown from outside.
5. Turn the cauliflower around to allow browning on all sides. Cook until cauliflower is still crunchy and not overcooked or soft.
6. Before serving, sprinkle a pinch of chilli powder and black salt if required. Serve hot.

Khatte Chhole

Serves 4

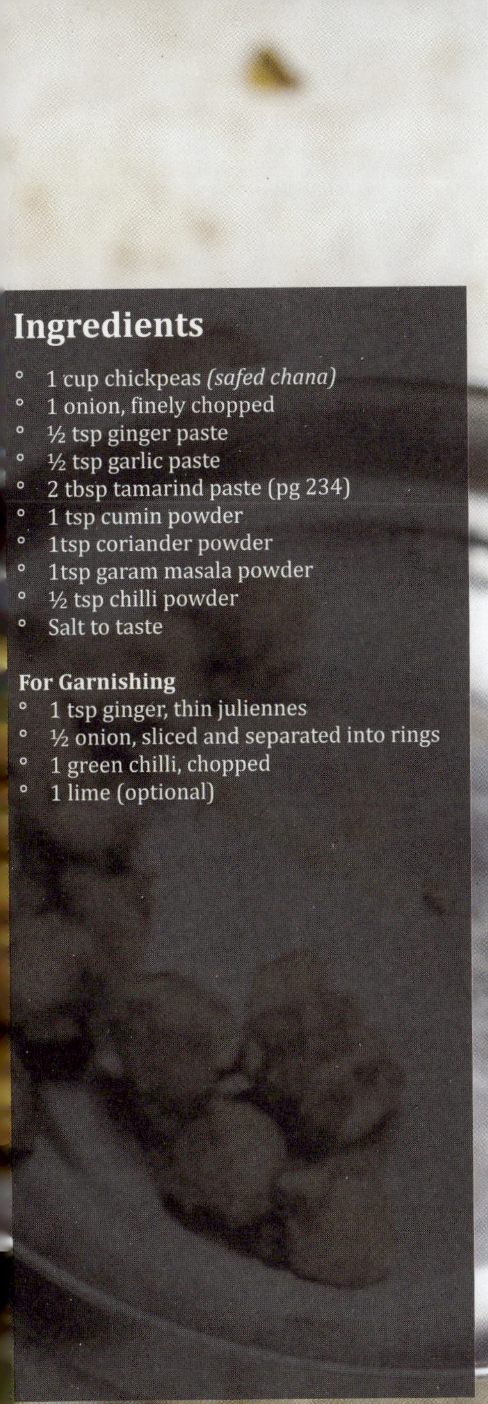

Ingredients

- 1 cup chickpeas *(safed chana)*
- 1 onion, finely chopped
- ½ tsp ginger paste
- ½ tsp garlic paste
- 2 tbsp tamarind paste (pg 234)
- 1 tsp cumin powder
- 1tsp coriander powder
- 1tsp garam masala powder
- ½ tsp chilli powder
- Salt to taste

For Garnishing

- 1 tsp ginger, thin juliennes
- ½ onion, sliced and separated into rings
- 1 green chilli, chopped
- 1 lime (optional)

Method

1. Soak the chickpeas in water overnight.
2. Boil the chickpeas in 2 cups of water and salt to taste until soft enough to eat (should take about 45 minutes). The water should by now be reduced to about ½ a cup. Alternatively, you can pressure cook for 20-25 minutes or 6 whistles.
3. In a pan, sauté the onion, ginger and garlic until slightly brown. Sprinkle water if needed to avoid them sticking to the pan.
4. Add the chilli, cumin powder and coriander powder and continue to cook. Keep sprinkling water to keep the masala moist. Cook for 5-7 minutes until the masala turns aromatic.
5. Gently crush some of the chickpeas in the existing water taking care to keep most of it whole.
6. Add the chickpeas to the masala. Stir well and add the tamarind paste and garam masala powder and cook for 2 more minutes. Adjust the salt as needed.
7. Serve hot with the garnishing of ginger juliennes, chilli and onion rings. Squeeze a lime (if using) before serving.

Karari Bhindi

Serves 2

Ingredients

- 300g medium okra *(bhindi)*
- 4 tbsp chickpea powder *(besan)*
- Pinch of red chilli powder
- Salt to taste

Method

1. Preheat the oven to 190°C for 10 minutes.
2. Make sure the okra are completely dry and then slice them in long thin strips (approximately six strips from one okra).
3. Toss together with the *besan*, chilli powder and salt.
4. Immediately spread on to a parchment paper or silicone sheet on baking tray and bake for 5 minutes and then turn and bake for another 3-4 minutes till golden brown and crisp. Serve immediately.

Chef's Note: *The okra strips could release water very quickly so it is important to place it in the oven as soon as they are tossed with the dry ingredients.*

South Indian Lauki

Serves 4

Ingredients

- 1 medium bottle gourd *(lauki)*, unpeeled and cut into cubes to make 4 cups
- A pinch of turmeric powder
- A pinch of asafoetida *(heeng)*
- Salt to taste
- 2-3 dry red chillies, broken into small pieces
- 1 heaped tbsp sesame seeds *(til)*
- 1 tbsp split pigeon pea lentil *(toor daal)*
- 1 tsp whole coriander seeds
- 1 tsp fennel seeds *(saunf)*
- 2 peeled garlic pods, finely chopped (optional)
- 1/4 cup roasted peanuts
- ½ cup coriander leaves for garnish

Method

To Prepare Masala

1. In a small pan on medium heat, roast the red chillies, pigeon pea lentil, coriander seeds, fennel seeds and sesame seeds, adding one after the other in this order. Once the *daal* turns golden, remove, cool and grind everything coarsely.
2. Now add the roasted peanuts to the grinder. Grind all together to a coarse powder and keep aside.

For the Dish

3. Heat 1/2 a cup of water in a heavy-bottomed pan. Add turmeric, salt, garlic (if using) and asafoeitda. Bring to a boil.
4. Add the bottle gourd cubes, bring to a boil again and cover and cook on medium heat for 10 minutes (increase time for harder gourds if using those) until the pieces are soft but retain shape. Ensure that there is a little liquid remaining in the pan.
5. Add the masala powder to the pan with the cooked gourd pieces and mix well. The excess water will be absorbed by the powder. Add a little more water if necessary to coat the vegetables thoroughly. Cook for another 3-5 minutes.
6. Check for salt and garnish with coriander leaves before serving. This dish goes very well with rice and millets or millet *rotis.*

Chef's Note: *You can substitute bottle gourd with any other squash or gourd like ridge gourd, zucchini, pumpkin, butternut squash etc.*

Methi Malai Matar

Serves 4

Ingredients

- 8 cups fenugreek leaves *(methi)*, chopped and packed tight
- ¾ cup green peas, shelled
- 1 large onion, chopped
- ½" piece ginger
- 4 cloves garlic
- ½ tsp dry mango powder *(amchur)*
- ½ tsp cinnamon powder
- ½ tsp red chilli powder (optional)
- 2 tbsp plain cashew cream (pg 229)
- Salt to taste

Method

1. Steam cook the peas for 3-4 minutes till soft enough to eat but firm.
2. In a wok on medium heat, add the onions with a little salt and 1 tbsp of water to avoid sticking to the pan and stir and cook for 3-4 minutes till translucent.
3. Separately, grind ginger and garlic together into a paste and add to the onions. Stir and cook for another 3-4 minutes. If it sticks to the pan, add a little water.
4. Add the peas and fenugreek leaves and mix thoroughly with the paste. Now add the cinnamon, dry mango powder, red chilli powder (if using) and more salt if required. Mix well and cook covered for another 2-3 minutes.
5. Mix in the cashew cream at the end with the cooked vegetables and turn off the heat. Serve hot.

Sweet Potato and Apple Sabzi

Serves 4

Ingredients

- 2 medium-sized sweet potatoes
- 10-15 large spinach leaves, chopped
- 2 small apples, sliced lengthways in ¼" thick slices
- 1/8 tsp turmeric
- ½ tsp chilli powder
- 2 tsp coriander powder
- ½ tsp black mustard seeds
- 1 tbsp split bengal gram lentil *(chana daal)*
- ½ tsp cumin seeds
- A pinch of asafoetida *(heeng)*
- Salt to taste

Method

1. Steam cook the sweet potatoes till soft enough to eat. This would take 10-12 minutes depending on the size. Set aside to cool.
2. Chop the cooled sweet potatoes into 1" cubes without removing the peel.
3. In a wok, sauté the cumin seeds, mustard seeds and *chana daal* until the mustards seeds pop.
4. Add the sweet potatoes and spinach and toss for about 2-3 minutes. Add the turmeric, chilli powder, coriander powder, asafoetida and salt.
5. Mix thoroughly, cover and cook. Allow the spinach to wilt and cook on low heat for 3-4 minutes.
6. Remove cover and add the apple slices. If you find the vegetables are sticking to the pan, just sprinkle some water and cover and cook for another 3-5 minutes making sure the apples don't turn brown.
7. Serve hot with millet *rotis*.

Drumsticks with Rice Cream

Serves 4

Ingredients

- 2 long drumsticks

For the Rice and Coconut Cream

- 2 tbsp brown rice
- ¼ cup fresh coconut, grated
- 1 green chilli

For the Tempering

- 1 tsp split bengal gram lentil *(chana daal)*
- 1 tsp green lentils *(sabut moong daal)*
- 1 tsp black split lentil *(tukda urad daal)*
- 1 tsp cumin seeds
- 2 red dried chilli
- A pinch of asafoetida (heeng)
- ¼ cup curry leaves *(kadi patta)*
- Salt to taste

Method

1. Soak the rice in ½ a cup of water for 2 hours.
2. Grind the rice first as smooth as possible. Then add coconut and green chilli and grind again into a paste.
3. Cut the drumsticks into 3" long pieces and sprinkle salt and toss to coat evenly.
4. Steam the drumsticks over boiling water for 10-12 minutes and set aside.
5. Meanwhile cook the rice mixture in 1 cup water for approximately 7-8 minutes until the texture is creamy and rice is cooked. Depending on the variety of rice you use, this process may vary in time and water consumption, so make sure to keep it as a creamy consistency.
6. Sauté the tempering i.e. the daals, cumin seeds, red chilli, curry leaves and asafoetida till fragrance is released.
7. Fold in the drumsticks, rice cream, sautéed seasoning and salt. Stir well.
8. If the rice becomes too sticky, you may sprinkle a little water to get a creamy consistency. Serve immediately as the rice cream tends to dry up.

Andhra Style Green Banana

Serves 2

Ingredients

- 2 raw green bananas or plantains, peeled and cut into 1" thick slices
- 1 tbsp split green lentils *(moong daal tukda)*, soaked for 10 minutes
- 4 tbsp fresh coconut, grated
- ½ tsp ginger, grated
- 1 green chilli, slit into half lengthways
- 8 curry leaves *(kadi pattaa)*
- ¾ tsp mustard seeds
- 1 tsp split bengal gram lentil *(chana daal)*
- 1 tsp split black lentil *(tukda urad daal)*
- 1 tbsp roasted peanuts, ground coarsely (optional)
- Salt to taste

Method

1. In a pan, cook the green lentils and the bananas in 1 cup water and salt for 30 minutes till soft. Alternatively cook for 5 minutes in pressure cooker till 1 whistle.
2. In a heavy-bottomed wok, roast the mustard seeds and the remaining lentils until the mustard seeds pop.
3. Add the ginger, chilli and curry leaves and sauté for 1 minute on medium heat. Sprinkle 1-2 tbsp of water if necessary to prevent it from sticking.
4. Add the cooked banana mixture to the spices and turn gently on the pan to cover with spices making sure not to break the banana pieces.
5. Mix salt and cook for another 2-3 minutes.
6. In the end sprinkle the fresh grated coconut, mix well and turn off the heat.
7. Garnish with roasted peanuts (if using) to add crunch before serving. Serve hot.

Parmal with Fresh Coconut

Serves 4

Ingredients

- 8 pointed gourds *(parmal)*, peeled and cut into halves lengthways
- 1 tbsp black mustard seeds
- 10 curry leaves *(kadi patta)*
- ½ cup fresh coconut, grated
- 1 green chilli, split in half
- Salt to taste

Method

1. Roast the mustard seeds and the curry leaves and set aside.
2. In a pan, put 1/4 cup water and bring to a boil. Add the parmal, chilli and salt.
3. Lower the heat and let it steam in a covered pan for approximately 3-4 minutes until cooked but not too soft. The vegetable should retain its shape.
4. When soft, add the roasted mustard seeds and curry leaves. Stir together for about a minute and turn off the heat.
5. Sprinkle the grated coconut over the vegetables and keep covered for 5 minutes to steam. Serve hot.

Chef's Note: *Some parmals have very hard skin so we have recommended peeling. However, you can try it with the skin if it is soft enough to eat. It will be more nutritious. You can susbtitute parmal with tindli, tinda, baby pumpkins or any small squashes.*

Stuffed Karela Surprise

Serves 4

Method

1. Immerse the gourds in boiling water with some salt and cooking soda (if using) for 2-3 minutes until tender but firm. Do not overcook. Remove from water and allow to cool.
2. Cut off the ends of the cooled gourds, about ¼" each side, and scoop out the insides with a thin knife or a spoon making sure not to break the karela. Remove the seeds from the scoop and if desired, add them to the chopped vegetables.
3. Steam cook the chopped vegetables for 3-4 minutes till soft enough to eat but firm enough to retain their colour and shape.
4. Sauté the onions for 2-3 minutes till transparent in a heavy-bottomed wok. Sprinkle water, if needed, to prevent sticking to the pan. Add the steamed vegetables, salt and all the dry spices and mix thoroughly and cook on medium heat for 2-3 minutes.
5. Mash the vegetable mixture gently, add in the raisin paste (if using) and coriander and mix thoroughly.
6. Stuff the whole gourds with this mixture tightly.
7. Put the stuffed gourds in a pan. Sprinkle with water and cover the pan to allow them to cook in their own steam for about 10-12 minutes. Turn periodically.
8. Remove from pan and lay on a chopping board to cool slightly.
9. Holding the gourd firmly from one end, use a serrated knife to cut circular slices and serve as a side dish.

Chef's Note: *Cooking soda helps to retain the colour of the vegetable.*

Ingredients

2 medium-large bitter gourds *(karela)*
¼ tsp cooking soda (optional)
½ cup onion, finely chopped
1 cup mixed seasonal vegetables (potato, carrot, beans, cauliflower), finely diced
¼ tsp red chilli powder
¼ tsp raw mango powder *(amchur)*
¼ tsp roasted cumin powder
2 tbsp raisin paste (optional) (pg 233)
2 tbsp coriander leaves, chopped
Salt to taste

Kerala Tofu Pepper Fry

Serves 4

Ingredients

- 2 cups hard tofu, diced into ¾" cubes
- 2 onions, finely chopped
- 2 sticks 1" cinnamon
- 1 black cardamom
- 2 bay leaves
- ½ cup coconut, grated
- 1 tsp garam masala powder
- 1 tsp black peppercorns, roughly ground
- 1 tsp dried mango powder *(amchur)*
- ¼ cup curry leaves *(kadi patta)*
- Salt to taste

Method

1. Before cooking, sprinkle some salt on the onions and allow them to release their own water for 10 minutes to prevent sticking to the pan. Sauté the onions until slightly brown.
2. Cover with lid and let the onions steam in their own juices for 2-3 minutes. Sprinkle water if needed to prevent it from sticking to the pan.
3. Add the cinnamon, cardamom, bay leaves, *garam masala* powder and *amchur*. Stir fry until colour turns dark. Cover with lid again if the mixture gets too dry.
4. Add the grated coconut and pepper and continue to stir on the heat for about 5 minutes while intermittently sprinkling water to keep the masala moist.
5. Add the tofu, salt to taste and half of the curry leaves and stir for another 5 minutes (again sprinkling water if the mixture gets too dry).
6. When ready, garnish with the remaining curry leaves and serve hot.

DAALS & BEANS

Sambhar Masala Powder

Ingredients

- 7-8 dry red chillies
- 1 tsp split bengal gram lentil *(chana da*
- 1 tsp split black lentil *(tukda urad daal)*
- 2 tsp coriander seeds
- 1 tsp black pepper corns
- 1/2 tsp black mustard seeds
- 1/2 tsp cumin seeds
- 1/2 tsp turmeric powder

Method

1. Place a small heavy-bottomed pan on medium to high heat, add the red chillie and the two lentils and stir continuousl for 2 minutes till the lentils begin to em an aroma and begin to get slightly brow
2. Immediately add the coriander, pepper and mustard seeds while continuing to stir and roast till the latter starts to pop
3. Now add the cumin seeds, stir for a few seconds and switch off the heat and wai for a minute. Add the turmeric powder. This prevents the powder from burning
4. Allow to cool completely before grindin into a fine powder. Store and use for upt 3 months.

Quintessential South Indian Sambhar

Serves 6

Ingredients

- 3/4 cup split pigeon pea lentil *(arhar/toor daal)*
- 4 pieces medium sized okra *(bhindi)*
- 1 drumstick, chopped into 2" long pieces
- 4 pieces green beans, chopped into 2" long pieces
- 1/2 cup sliced carrot rounds
- 2 onions, one cut four ways and one chopped finely
- 2 tomatoes, chopped finely
- 2 tbsp tamarind paste (pg 234)
- 1 aubergine/brinjal, 1" cubed
- 8 curry leaves *(kadi patta)*
- 2 dry whole red chillies
- 1 tsp black mustard seeds
- 1/2 tsp turmeric
- Pinch of asafoetida *(heeng)* powder
- 2 tbsp sambhar masala powder*
- Salt to taste

**You can buy 'sambhar masala powder' in any Indian grocery store or like us, you may want to make it from scratch.*

Method

1. Soak *daal* in 4 cups of water for 2 hours.
2. Boil the soaked *daal* with the turmeric, salt, onion and tomatoes until half cooked which should take approximately ½ hour in a pan or if using a pressure cooker, 1 whistle.
3. Add all the chopped vegetables and further cook for about 10 minutes until vegetables are done.
4. In a separate pan roast the mustard seeds, whole red chillies and curry leaves until the mustard seeds start to pop. Turn off the heat and add in sambhar powder and asafoetida powder stirring for 1 minute.
5. Pour this spice mixture on the *daal* and stir well. Add the tamarind paste and adjust the salt. Cook for another 2 minutes. Serve hot with idli (pg 27), dosa (pg 29) or rice.

Arhar Daal with Raw Mango

Serves 4

Ingredients

- 3/4 cup split pigeon pea lentil *(arhar daal)*
- 4 okra *(bhindi)* chopped into 2-3 big pieces each
- 1 large tomato, sliced into 8 and then halved
- 1 raw mango, sliced length ways
- Pinch of asafoetida *(heeng)*
- ½ tsp cumin seeds
- 1 red dried chilli, whole
- ¼ tsp turmeric
- Salt to taste

Method

1. Boil the daal in 2 cups water with the turmeric and salt in a pot. Once it reaches boiling point, turn the heat to low, cover the pot and let it simmer for 10 minutes until daal is soft.
2. Add the tomatoes, mango and okra and cook for 5 more minutes.
3. In a separate pan roast the cumin seeds, red chilli and asafoetida until a fragrance is released and sprinkle over the daal. Serve hot.

All Time Favourite Daal Makhani

Serves 4-6

Ingredients

- ¾ cup black gram lentil *(sabut urad daal)* soaked for 2 hours
- 1/2 cup plain cashew cream (pg 229)
- 1 onion, finely chopped
- 1/2 tomato, finely chopped
- ½ tsp ginger paste
- ½ tsp garlic paste
- ½ tsp chilli powder
- ½ tsp cumin powder
- ½ tsp coriander powder
- 2 slices of tomato for garnish
- Salt to taste

Method

1. Boil the daal with salt in 3 cups of water for 30 minutes or until soft. Alternatively, pressure cook with 2 cups water till 3 whistles. Check to ensure the daal gets mashed between your fingers and there are no hard bits. At this stage the daal should be slightly split. Retain the boiling water.
2. In a pan, sauté the onions, ginger and garlic till slightly brown sprinkling some water to prevent sticking and burning. This would take approximately 4-6 minutes on medium heat.
3. Add the tomatoes, all the dry spices and cook for 5-7 minutes until spices release a fragrance. Check salt to taste.
4. Remove one cup of daal and gently mash it with the back of a spoon to give thickness. Add the mashed and remaining daal with the water to the tomato gravy. Bring to a boil and turn off the heat.
5. Stir in the cashew cream to give richness to the daal. Garnish with tomato slices and serve hot with rice or roti.

North Eastern Chana Daal

Serves 4

Ingredients

- 1 cup split bengal gram lentil *(chana daal)*
- ¼ tsp turmeric
- 2 pc black cardamom
- 2 bay leaves
- 2" stick cinnamon
- 1 red dried chilli
- ¼ tsp cumin seeds
- 2 tbsp diced fresh coconut
- 1 tsp raisin paste (pg 233)
- Salt to taste

Method

1. Soak the daal for 3 hours.
2. Cook the daal, turmeric and salt in a pressure cooker with 2 cups of water till one whistle or for 1/2 hour in a pan with 21/2 cups water.
3. Roast all the spices and coconut in a separate pan until fragrance is released.
4. Add the daal and the raisin paste to the pan and cook for 5 minutes. The daal should have a creamy consistency, yet not absolutely mushy. Serve hot.

Delicious Sookhi Moong Daal

Serves 4

Ingredients

- 1 cup split dehusked mung beans *(dhuli moong daal)*
- ¼ tsp turmeric
- 2 onions, chopped
- 1 tsp garlic, chopped
- 1 onion, thinly sliced
- 2 tomatoes, chopped
- 2 tbsp fresh coriander leaves, chopped
- 1 green chilli, chopped
- Salt to taste

Method

1. Boil the daal with 2 cups water, salt and turmeric for approximately 10 minutes untill 3/4 cooked and drain off the excess water.
2. Sauté the sliced onions without oil till golden brown and crispy. Alternatively, you can crisp them in the oven by grilling on 1800C for 5-6 minutes. Keep aside for garnishing.
3. Sauté the chopped onions and garlic till brown and soft. Sprinkle water to prevent it from sticking to the pan. Add the chopped tomatoes and green chilli and after 1 minute add the daal.
4. Stir for another minute, adjust salt to taste and serve hot with crispy golden onions and chopped coriander leaves on top.

Maharashtra Style Lobiya

Serves 4

Ingredients

- ½ cup black eyed peas *(lobiya)*
- 1 cup zucchini, chopped
- ¼ cup coconut, grated
- 2 tbsp tamarind paste (pg 234)
- 2 kashmiri red chillies
- 1 tsp fenugreek *(methi)* seeds
- Salt to taste

Method

1. Soak the black eyed peas for 6 hours or overnight. Discard the water and pressure cook with 2 cups fresh water and salt for 8-10 minutes or 4 whistles.
2. In a small pan roast the red chillies for 2 minutes and when almost done add the fenugreek seeds and roast for another minute. Allow to cool.
3. In a small grinder add the roasted spices, and grind to a coarse powder. Add the coconut and tamarind paste and grind together to form a smooth paste using a little water if necessary to move the blades.
4. In a large saucepan, add the cooked beans along with its water and the zucchini. Cook on high heat for 2-3 minutes till the water comes to a boil.
5. Lower the heat, add the paste made in step 3 and mix thoroughly. Cook covered for another 3-5 minutes till the zucchini has softened a little.
6. Serve hot with rice or *roti*.

Chef's Note: *You can substitute zucchini with bottle gourd, pumpkin or kohlrabi. You can increase the amount of vegetables as per your liking. The more the vegetables, the healthier the dish will be!*

Family Favourite Rajma

Serves 6

Ingredients

- 1 cup kidney beans *(rajma)*
- 4 cups water
- 1 medium tomato, diced
- 1 onion, chopped
- 1 tsp ginger paste
- 1 tsp garlic paste
- 1/2 tsp cumin *(jeera)* powder
- 2 large black cardamoms
- 2 sticks cinnamon
- 2 dried bay leaves
- 1 tsp coriander powder
- ½ tsp red chilli powder
- 2 tbsp fresh coriander leaves, chopped
- Salt to taste

Method

1. Soak the kidney beans overnight. Drain out the soaking water and wash again.
2. Add 4 cups water and pressure cook on medium heat for 4-5 whistles. Retain the water.
3. In a pan dry roast the cardamoms, cinnamon and bay leaves, stirring constantly to avoid burning, till they emit an aroma.
4. Then add the tomatoes, onion, ginger, garlic, coriander powder, jeera powder, red chilli powder. Sprinkle water if the masala sticks to the pan. Cook for 8-10 minutes, stirring intermittently.
5. Add the boiled kidney beans including the water into the paste and crush some of the beans roughly to give thickness to the gravy. Add salt to taste and bring to a rolling boil for 2 minutes.
6. Garnish with fresh coriander leaves before serving.

GRAINS

Rice and Millets

Roti and Bread

Jackfruit Biryani

Serves 4

Ingredients

- 1½ cups brown rice, soaked for 4-6 hours
- 500g raw jackfruit *(kathal)*, diced into 1 ½" chunks
- 3 medium onions, sliced lengthways
- 2 medium onions, ground to a paste
- 2 large tomatoes, ground to a paste
- 1 stick cinnamon
- 2 black cardamoms
- 2 bay leaves
- 1 tsp cumin powder
- 1 tsp coriander powder
- ½ tsp turmeric powder
- ½ tsp chilli powder
- 1 tsp garlic paste
- 1 tsp ginger paste
- Salt to taste
- ¼ tsp saffron threads
- ½ cup fresh coriander leaves, chopped (optional)

Method

1. In 3 cups of water, boil the rice for 20 minutes or till cooked.
2. Sauté the sliced onions until browned. Sprinkle water if needed to avoid it from sticking to the pan. Set aside 2 tbsp for the garnish.
3. Sauté the onion, ginger and garlic pastes. Add cinnamon, coriander and cumin powders and bay leaves. Cook for 3-4 minutes on medium heat, till golden brown. Sprinkle some water if needed to prevent sticking to the pan.
4. Add the tomato paste, turmeric, salt and chilli powder. Cook for about 3-4 minutes until aroma is released from the *masala*. Add 2 cups of water and the jackfruit and bring to a boil. Cover and simmer for 15 minutes until the gravy is thick and jackfruit is thoroughly cooked and soft.
5. Take a large pan and spread a layer of rice evenly on the bottom. Top with 1/3 of the sliced and sautéed onion, saffron and fresh coriander.
6. Now add a layer of the jackfruit curry.
7. Repeat the layers twice more starting with the rice so you have three layers in total.
8. Cover the pan with a tight fitting lid and place the pan on a hot griddle or *tawa* and allow to steam for 10 minutes.
9. Garnish with the sautéed onions kept aside and fresh chopped coriander (if using).

Chef's Note: *The pan needs to be placed on the tawa and not direct heat to prevent the bottom layer of the rice from burning.*

Different qualities of rice take different times to cook. One method of checking whether the rice is cooked is to press one grain between your fingers and ensure it is soft from inside.

Traditional Lemon Rice

Serves 4

Ingredients

For the Rice

- 1 cup brown rice, soaked for 4-6 hours
- 11/2 cups mixed vegetables, julienned (carrot, green capsicum, onion, cabbage)
- 3 tbsp lemon juice
- Salt to taste
- 1 green chilli (optional)

For Tempering

- 1 tbsp split bengal gram lentils *(chana daal)*
- 1/2 tsp mustard seeds
- 2 tbsp curry leaves *(kadi patta)*
- 2 dry red chillies
- 1/2 tsp turmeric powder

Method

1. In 3 cups of water, boil the rice for 20 minutes or till cooked.
2. Roast the *chana daal* until brown and then add the rest of the tempering ingredients except turmeric powder. When the mustard seeds pop, turn off the heat, add turmeric powder and stir for 1 minute.
3. Turn on the heat, add all the vegetables and salt to the tempering and stir for 2-3 minutes. Do not overcook the vegetables. As they are finely julienned they just need a little steam to soften.
4. Add the rice and lemon juice and mix well without breaking the rice grains. Adjust the salt if necessary.
5. Garnish with a green chilli (if using). Serve hot.

Chef's Note: *Different qualities of rice take different times to cook. One method of checking whether the rice is cooked is to press one grain between your fingers and ensure it is soft from inside.*

Hara Bhara Pulao

Serves 4

Ingredients

- 1 cup brown rice, soaked for 4-6 hours
- 3 cups mixed green vegetables, chopped (any 4 of your choice from beans, broccoli, green capsicum, peas, spinach or zucchini)
- 1 black cardamom
- 2 cloves
- 1 bay leaf
- 1 stick cinnamon
- 1/2 tsp cumin seeds
- 1 mace *(javitri)*, the inside netted part (optional)
- Salt to taste

Method

1. Place a large pan on medium heat, roast the cardamom, cinnamon, cloves, cumin seeds, mace and bay leaf until fragrance is released.
2. Drain the water from the rice and add the rice to the pan and fold in the spices. Add 2 cups of water to the rice and bring to a boil.
3. Reduce the heat and add all the vegetables and salt to the rice. Let it simmer until the water is fully absorbed into the rice. This should take about 15-20 minutes. Serve hot with peanut curd (pg 223).

Chef's Note: *Different qualities of rice take different times to cook. One method of checking whether the rice is cooked is to press one grain between your fingers and ensure it is soft from inside.*

Cooling Curd Rice

Serves 4

Ingredients

For the Rice

- ½ cup brown rice, soaked for 4-6 hours or 1 cup leftover cooked brown rice
- 1 cup thick peanut curd (pg 224), whisked
- ¼ cup carrots, grated
- ¼ cup cucumber or zucchini, grated
- Salt to taste
- ¼ tsp green chillies, chopped (optional)

For Tempering

- 1 tsp split bengal gram lentils *(chana daal)*
- 1 tsp split black gram lentils *(tukda urad daal)*
- 1 dried red chilli, whole
- ¼ tsp mustard seeds
- ¼ tsp cumin
- ½ tsp ginger, minced
- 5-6 curry leaves *(kadi patta)*
- Pinch of asafoetida *(heeng)*

Method

1. Discard the soaking water of the rice and add 11/4 cups fresh water. Boil the rice for 20 minutes or until cooked.
2. Allow to cool completely. If required in a rush, spread it on a plate for rapid cooling.
3. Put the cooled rice in a bowl and mix in the whisked curd, salt to taste, the grated vegetables and green chillies (if using)
4. Prepare the tempering by heating a small pan and adding the two lentils first and roast for 1 minute or till it releases an aroma. Now add the chilli, mustard seeds and cumin. Stir and roast till the mustard seeds pop. Add the ginger and curry leaves and stir for 1-2 minutes. Sprinkle a little water to prevent the ginger from sticking to the pan. Add the asafoetida and turn off the heat.
5. Spread over the curd rice and mix before eating. It's best to eat this fresh and not store it in the fridge.

Chef's note: *This dish is usually eaten in South Indian homes at the end of a meal. It is often made with leftover cooked rice. You can make the rice ahead of time to allow it to cool completely.*

Foxtail Millet Bisi Bele Bhaat

Serves 4

Ingredients

For the Rice

- ½ cup foxtail millet *(kangni)*
- ½ cup split pigeon pea lentils *(arhar daal)*
- 1 cup mixed seasonal vegetables (carrots, beans, turnip, peas), diced
- Salt to taste

For Tempering

- ½ tsp mustard seeds
- Pinch of asafoetida *(heeng)*
- 2 tbsp curry leaves *(kadi patta)*
- 2 dry red chillies
- 1 tomato, finely chopped
- 1 onion, finely chopped

1 tbsp Sambhar Masala Powder (Pg 124)

For Garnishing

- 6-7 fox nuts *(makhana)*, roasted (optional)
- ¼ cup fresh coriander leaves, chopped
- 2-3 red chillies

Method

1. Place the millets and lentils in a pan with 2 cups of water and bring to a boil.
2. Add the vegetables and simmer for 8-10 minutes or till millets are soft and cooked.
3. In a pan, roast the mustard and chillies until the seeds begin to pop. Add rest of the tempering ingredients and stir until aroma is released.
4. Add the *sambhar* powder to the tempering. Mix well.
5. Finally add this masala to the cooked millets, mix well and turn off the heat.
6. Add the garnishing on top just before serving hot.

Ellu Sadam Black Sesame Rice

Serves 4

Ingredients

For the Rice

- 1 cup brown rice, soaked for 4-6 hours
- Salt to taste

For Grinding

- 2 tsp split black gram lentil *(tukda urad daal)*
- ½ tsp pepper corns
- 2 red chillies (optional)
- 7-8 fresh or dried curry leaves *(kadi patta)*
- 2 tsp black sesame seeds *(kaale til)*
- Salt to taste

For Seasoning

- ½ tsp split bengal gram lentils *(chana daal)*
- ½ tsp split black gram lentils *(tukda urad daal)*
- ¼ tsp mustard seeds
- 2 tbsp peanuts, roasted
- ¼ cup cashews nuts, roasted
- 2 red chillies
- 6-7 curry leaves *(kadi patta)*
- ½ tsp black sesame seeds
- Pinch of asafoetida *(heeng)*

Method

1. Discard the soaking water. Boil the rice with 2¼ times fresh water and salt for 20 minutes or until cooked. Set aside.
2. In a pan over medium heat, roast the ingredients for grinding, adding the sesame seeds as the last ingredient. When the sesame seeds start to pop, remove from heat. Allow to cool completely and then grind into a fine powder.
3. Add about 3-4 tsp of the ground masala to the rice and mix well. This powder can be quite spicy so adjust to your taste. Check the salt at this stage too and add more if required.
4. For the seasoning, roast the two lentils and mustards seeds until they are golden brown. This should take about 3-4 minutes. Add in the cashew nuts, curry leaves and red chillies and continue to stir and roast for 1-2 minutes. Now add the roasted peanuts and finally add the sesame seeds and roast for another minute. After turning off the heat, add the asafoetida and stir.
5. Sprinkle this roasted mixture all over the rice and gently mix it into the rice. Serve hot.

Chef's Note: *Different qualities of rice take different times to cook. One method of checking whether the rice is cooked is to press one grain between your fingers and ensure it is soft from inside.*

Cauliflower 'Rice' Biryani

Serves 4-6

Ingredients

For the Rice

- 1 cauliflower
- 1 bay leaf
- 1 cinnamon stick
- 2 black cardamoms
- 1 onion, finely sliced
- 4 sticks of green beans, trimmed and cut into 2" length
- 1 carrot, cut into sticks or batons
- ½ red bell pepper, deseeded, thinly sliced
- ½ cup of fresh peas
- 1 tsp chilli powder, or more to taste
- 1 garlic clove, chopped
- 1/2" thick ginger piece, finely sliced
- 1/2 tsp turmeric powder
- 2 tomatoes, chopped
- 1 cup coriander leaves, chopped
- 10 cashews, roasted
- Salt to taste

Method

1. Cut the cauliflower into individual florets and place the florets in a food processor. Process until broken down into small pieces but make sure not to make a mash.
2. Dry roast the cardamoms, cinnamon stick and bay leaves in a pan on medium heat stirring until aromatic.
3. Stir in the onions and cook for 5 minutes until nicely golden brown. Sprinkle water if needed to prevent it from sticking to the pan.
4. Add the beans, carrots, peas, chilli, garlic, ginger, turmeric and salt. Place a lid on the pan and continue to cook for 10 minutes on low heat, stirring from time to time to prevent burning.
5. Stir in the cauliflower, bell pepper and tomatoes and cook for 3 minutes ensuring that the 'rice' does not overcook and become mushy. Turn off the heat and mix in the coriander leaves.
6. Taste the biryani, adjusting the seasoning and adding more coriander if needed, then place in a large serving dish. Top with the roasted cashews before serving.

Rustic Bajra Khichdi

Serves 4

Ingredients

- 1/2 cup broken pearl millet *(bajra)*
- ½ cup red lentils *(masoor daal)*
- 2 cups bottle gourd – cut into 1" cubes
- 1 onion, cut into quarters and opened
- 1 black cardamom
- 2 bay leaves
- 1 stick cinnamon
- ½ tsp whole black pepper corn
- ¼ tsp turmeric
- Salt to taste

Method

1. Sprinkle the onions with ¼ tsp salt, mix and set aside for 5-7 minutes to release its own water so it will not stick while cooking.
2. In a pan, roast the bay leaves, cinnamon, cardamom and peppercorns till they emit an aroma.
3. Add the onions and stir and cook for 4-5 minutes till onions are slightly brown. Add the turmeric and stir for 1-2 minutes.
4. Now add all the remaining ingredients together in the pan with 2 cups of water. Allow the khichdi to come to a boil on high heat.
5. As soon as it boils, lower the heat and simmer, covered with a lid for approximately 30 minutes.
6. Check if khichdi is cooked by pressing a grain between your fingers as you would do for a rice grain.
7. When ready, serve hot. You can pair this with a chutney or peanut curd (pg 224).

Amaranth Aaloo Parantha

Makes 4-6

Ingredients

- 1 cup amaranth flour
- 1 cup potatoes, steamed and mashed
- ½ cup peas, steamed
- ½ tsp ginger paste
- 1 tbsp fresh coriander, finely chopped
- ¼ tsp pepper, coarsely ground
- Salt to taste

Method

1. Knead together all the ingredients using a little water if needed till you have a tight ball of dough.
2. Separate into 4-6 equal balls depending on the size of the parantha preferred.
3. Use your hands to flatten the dough ball and use some dry flour to roll out the parantha.
4. Cook on medium heat on a flat griddle or *tawa*, turning the parantha after a few minutes till both sides are cooked well. This takes a little longer to cook and it is important not to raise the heat and allow the middle portion to be cooked properly. So be patient.
5. Enjoy with curd (pg 224) and Sweet Ambol Chutneys (pg 215).

Makki ki Roti

Makes 3 rotis

Ingredients

- 1 cup yellow corn flour *(makki atta)*
- ½ tsp carom seed or bishop's weed *(ajwain)*
- ½ cup fresh fenugreek or coriander leaves finely chopped
- Salt to taste

Method

1. Mix all the ingredients together.
2. Add ½ cup warm water to knead the dough into a tight ball.
3. Divide into 3 portions and roll into balls using a little dry flour.
4. Wet 2 plain cloth napkins and wring them to almost dry. Place the ball in the centre of the wet napkin and flatten using your hands. Put the other wet napkin on top and gently spread and flatten with a rolling pin in all directions to get a nice round shape. Roll it as much you can without breaking it.
5. Use an upturned pan/ lid to mark and remove the uneven edges.
6. Put a flat skillet (or Indian *tawa*) on high heat till very hot and gently lay the rolled out roti taking care to spread it flat.
7. Allow to cook on medium heat on one side for 3-5 minutes. Check the underside to ensure a little browning and flip over to the other side. Allow to cook for another 2-3 minutes till slightly browned.
8. Serve hot with Coconut Butter (pg 227).

Garlic Missi Roti

Makes 4 rotis

Ingredients

- 1 cup chickpea flour *(besan)*
- 1 cup sorghum *(jowar)* flour
- 1 tbsp garlic, grated
- 1 tbsp green chillies, minced
- Salt to taste

Method

1. Mix all the ingredients together. Add ½ cup warm water to knead the dough. Add more as needed to form a tight ball.
2. Divide into 4 parts and roll into balls using a little dry flour.
3. Roll and flatten with a rolling pin in all directions to achieve a nice round shape. Roll it as much as you can without breaking it.
4. If it goes out of shape, you can use an upturned pan/lid to mark and remove the uneven edges.
5. Put a flat skillet (or Indian *tawa*) on high heat till very hot and gently put the rolled out dough taking care to spread it flat.
6. Allow to cook on medium heat on one side for 3-5 minutes,. Check the underside to ensure a little browning and flip over to the other side. Allow to cook for another 2-3 minutes till slightly browned.
7. Serve hot when ready to eat.

Jowar Bhakri with Coriander

Makes 3

Ingredients

- 1 cup sorghum *(jowar)* flour
- ½ cup fresh coriander or dill, chopped
- Salt to taste
- Fresh cracked pepper

Method

1. Add the sorghum in a pan and add ½-1 cup (as needed) boiling water, enough to form a dough. Stir with a spoon to make the dough.
2. When cool enough to touch, mix in the remaining ingredients.
3 Immediately, divide into 3 parts and roll into balls using a little dry flour.
4. Wet 2 plain cloth napkins and wring them to almost dry. Place the ball in the centre of the wet napkin and flatten using your hands. Put the other wet napkin on top and gently spread and flatten with a rolling pin in all directions to achieve a nice round shape. Roll it as much as you can without breaking it.
5. Use an upturned pan/ lid to mark and remove the uneven edges.
6. Put a flat skillet (or Indian *tawa*) on high heat till very hot and gently put the rolled out dough taking care to spread it flat.
7. On medium heat, allow to cook on one side for 3-5 minutes. Spread a spoonful of water on the top side to keep it moist.
8. Check the underside to ensure a little browning and flip over to the other side. Allow to cook for another 2-3 minutes till slightly browned.
9. Serve hot with a dollop of coconut butter. (pg 227)

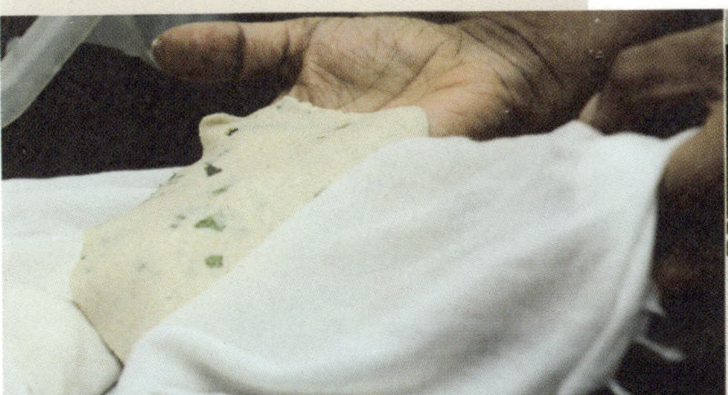

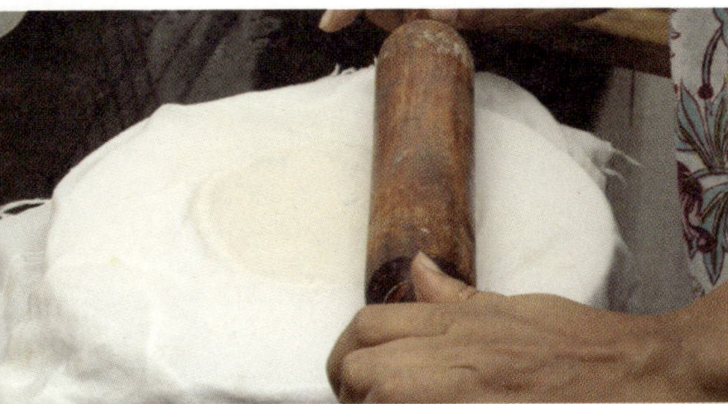

Ingredients

For the Bread

- 1/2 cup dehusked split green lentil *(dhuli moong daal)*
- 1/2 cup dehusked split black gram lentil *(dhuli urad daal)*

For the Masala and Topping

- ½ onion, sliced lengthways
- ¼ cup sun dried tomatoes, chopped
- 1tsp garlic, chopped, toasted to crispy
- 3 tsp dried fenugreek leaves *(kasuri methi)*, crushed (substitute with dried oregano or thyme)
- 1 ½ tsp onion seeds *(kalonji)*
- Salt to taste
- 1 tbsp white sesame seeds *(safed til)*

Steamed Masala Bread

Makes 1 loaf

Method

1. Soak the two lentils separately for 4-5 hours. Grind them separately and then mix together in a large bowl for fermenting overnight for 10-12 hours. The warmer the ambient temperature, lesser the time needed. Be careful not to over ferment as it might start to smell putrid.
2. When the fermented paste is ready, prepare the masala ingredients. Roast the sesame seeds in a small pan on medium heat for 4-5 minutes stirring constantly till light brown in colour. Sauté the sliced onions till browned. Sprinkle a few drops of water to prevent sticking to the pan.
3. Mix together all the masala ingredients. Mix 2/3 of the masala into the fermented batter keeping aside 1/3 for the topping.
4. Pour the batter in a loaf dish for steaming. Sprinkle the remaining masala topping over the loaf.
5. Steam cook over boiling water for about 45 minutes until a knife inserted into the loaf comes out clean – as you would check a cake.
6. Allow to cool before slicing. This bread also makes wonderful toast.

Chef's Note - *This recipe can also be used to make a plain bread by skipping the masala and topping ingredients.*

ANYTIME SNACKS

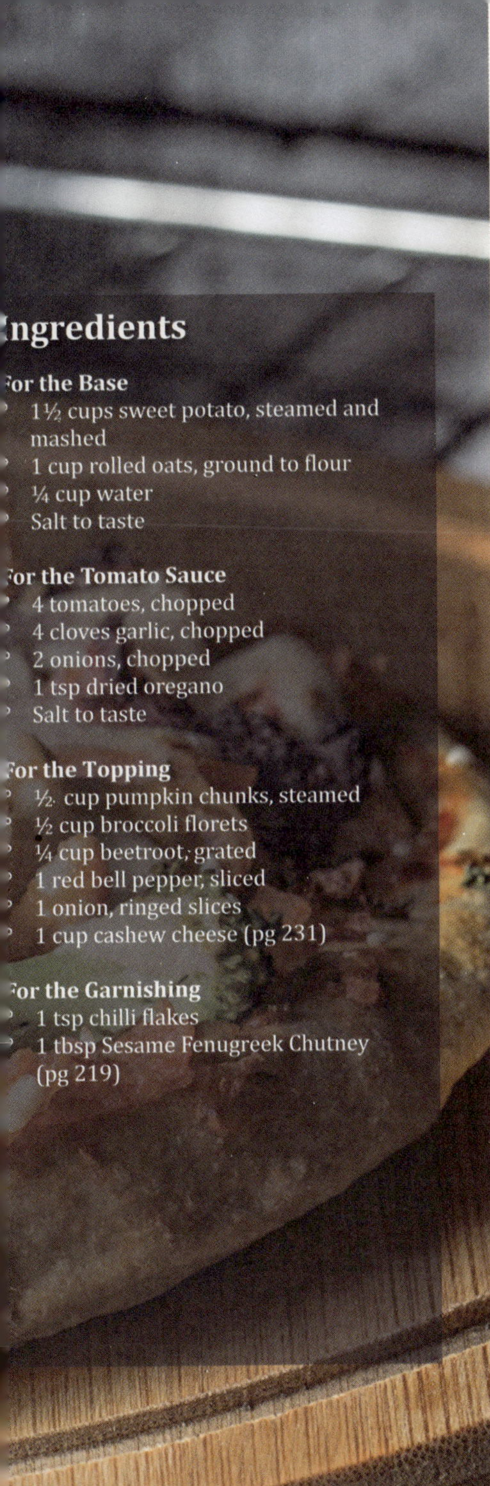

Ingredients

For the Base

- 1½ cups sweet potato, steamed and mashed
- 1 cup rolled oats, ground to flour
- ¼ cup water
- Salt to taste

For the Tomato Sauce

- 4 tomatoes, chopped
- 4 cloves garlic, chopped
- 2 onions, chopped
- 1 tsp dried oregano
- Salt to taste

For the Topping

- ½ cup pumpkin chunks, steamed
- ½ cup broccoli florets
- ¼ cup beetroot, grated
- 1 red bell pepper, sliced
- 1 onion, ringed slices
- 1 cup cashew cheese (pg 231)

For the Garnishing

- 1 tsp chilli flakes
- 1 tbsp Sesame Fenugreek Chutney (pg 219)

Fiery Indian Pizza

Make 2 pizzas

Method

1. To prepare the base, place the sweet potato mash, oat flour and salt in a mixing bowl. Gradually add the water to make a dough by kneading it to a smooth consistency so it is easy to roll into a pizza base.
2. Divide the dough in 2 halves. Sprinkle some oat flour before rolling out the base on a silicone or parchment paper sheet. You may need to spread the dough with the palms of your hands if the rolling is difficult. Spread the pizza base as thin as possible without breaking.
3. Place the base on a baking tray and prick with a fork in 6-8 places so the dough doesn't rise. Cook at 190°C for ½ hour until the bottom is slightly brown and edges are crisp. Depending on the oven, you may need to flip and cook on both sides.
4. Prepare the tomato sauce by adding the chopped onions and garlic in a wok and stirring and cooking for 4-5 minutes till translucent. Now add the remaining sauce ingredients and cook covered for 5 minutes to soften the tomatoes. Then uncover and cook for another 5-7 minutes, allowing the water to evaporate and the paste to be thickened.
5. Spread the tomato paste generously on the pizza base. Place the pumpkin chunks, broccoli florets, red pepper, beetroot and onion rings evenly on the base.
6. Place spoonfuls of the cashew cheese over the pizza evenly.
7. Grill the pizza on 200°C for 5-7 minutes until slightly brown on top.
8. Before serving, garnish with chilli flakes and sesame chutney for the distinctly Indian touch.

Chef's Note: *Since sweet potatoes vary in size and variety, you can steam them whole or chopped for 10-15 minutes depending on size, till completely soft. When slightly cooled, mash the sweet potatoes thoroughly with a fork or in a food processor.*

Street-smart Dahi Vada

Makes 14-16 vadas

Ingredients

- 1 cup black-eyed beans *(lobiya)*, soaked overnight
- 1 tsp ginger, grated
- ½ green chilli, chopped (optional)
- ½ cup bottle gourd *(lauki)*, grated
- Salt to taste
- 3 cups rice and peanut curd, whipped (Pg 224)
- 6 tbsp green chutney (Pg 214)
- 8 tbsp date and tamarind chutney (Pg 216)
- Red chilli powder to taste (optional)
- Black salt to taste
- ½ tsp black pepper powder
- 1 tsp roasted cumin powder
- 2 tbsp fresh coriander, chopped
- 4 tbsp pomegranate arils for garnish

Method

1. In a stone or regular grinder, add the soaked and drained beans, ginger, green chilli and salt. Grind to a coarse texture. Use as little water as necessary to move the blades to form a thick batter.
2. Stir and mix in the grated bottle gourd into this batter.
3. Scoop this mix into *idli* moulds and steam in the *idli* steamer for 25-30 minutes or till a knife inserted comes out clean.
4. Once cooked, cool the vadas to room temperature.
5. In the curd, mix black salt, black pepper and ½ tsp roasted cumin powder and whip to a smooth consistency.
6. Pour over the vadas and dress with the chopped coriander, pomegranate, the 2 chutneys and a sprinkle of cumin powder and red chilli if using.

Purani Dilli ki Pakora Chaat

Serves 4

Ingredients

For the Pakoras

- 1 cup chickpea flour *(besan)*
- 1 tbsp peanut butter (Pg 228)
- 2 onions, finely chopped
- 1 green chilli , finely chopped
- 1 tbsp fresh coriander, chopped
- ¼ tsp baking powder
- ½ cup water
- Salt to taste

For the Radish Chutney

- ½ cup radish, grated
- 1 tbsp lime juice
- ½ tsp black or regular salt
- 1 tsp fresh coriander, finely chopped
- 1 tsp green chilli, finely sliced (optional)

Green Chutney (pg 214)
Date and Tamarind Chutney (pg 216)

Method

1. To make the fritters or pakoras, mix all the ingredients together adding the water as required to form small-sized balls. Flatten the balls a little without breaking.
2. Bake in the oven at 200°C for 35 minutes turning the pakoras at half time.
3. For the radish chutney, combine all the ingredients. Make sure the taste is tangy and sharp.
4. Serve the pakoras with the three chutneys and sprinkle some chopped coriander and sliced green chillies on top.

Chilli Cheese Toast

Makes 6 toasts

Ingredients

- ½ steamed masala bread (pg 165)
- 1 tbsp onion, finely chopped
- 2 tbsp tomatoes, finely chopped
- 1 tbsp yellow pepper, finely chopped
- 1 tsp green chilli, finely chopped
- 1tsp fresh coriander, finely chopped
- Salt to taste
- ½ tsp watermelon seeds for garnishing

For the Watermelon Seed Cheese

- 1 cup watermelon seeds, soaked for 6 hours
- 2 cloves of garlic
- 1 tsp mixed herbs (fresh or dried)
- Black pepper powder to taste
- Salt to taste
- 1 tsp psyllium husk *(isabgul)* powder (optional)

Method

1. Grind together the cheese ingredients except psyllium husk, using as little water as needed to move the blades. If you need the cheese to be thicker, remove from the grinder and mix in the psyllium husk.
2. Combine the cheese with the chopped onion, 1 tbsp tomatoes, yellow pepper, coriander, green chilli and salt.
3. Slice the bread and toast the slices until crisp. Top with the cheese and grill at 200° C for 5 minutes or till slightly brown.
4. Decorate with the rest of the tomatoes and the melon seeds and a little more salt and pepper. Serve hot.

Chef's Note: *Watermelon seed cheese is an acquired taste. To mellow it down, you can substitute half the amount with cashews and follow the same recipe. Else, you can substitute with cashew cheese (pg 231).*

Mumbai Sev Puri

Serves 4

Ingredients

- 1 cucumber
- ½ carrot, grated
- ½ cup potatoes, boiled, mashed and salted
- ¼ cup peanuts, roasted
- ½ cup sprouts
- 1 tsp red chilli flakes
- ½ tsp roasted cumin powder
- Black salt to taste
- ¼ cup peanut curd, whipped (pg 223)
- ¼ cup tamarind and date chutney (pg 216)
- ¼ cup green coriander and mint chutney (pg 214)

Method

1. Cut ½ cm thick round slices of the cucumber without peeling.
2. Scoop a little mashed potato on top of each cucumber slice and push in one peanut in the centre of the potato mash.
3. Top with sprouts and some grated carrots to give the effect of *'sev'.*
4. Whisk the curd with cumin, salt and chillies.
5. Drizzle it on top of the cucumber roundels along with a couple of drops each of green chutney and tamarind chutney.
6. Garnish with a little cumin and chili flakes before serving.

Sweet Potato Country Fries

Serves 4

Ingredients

- 6 medium-large sweet potatoes
- ¼ cup thick coconut milk
- 1 tsp mixed dried herbs or dried mint
- 1 tsp garlic powder
- Salt and pepper to taste

Method

1. Mix coconut milk, herbs, salt and pepper
2. Slice the sweet potatoes lengthwise keeping the skin intact and marinate with coconut milk mixture for 15-20 minutes mixing well so all the sweet potato slices are coated well.
3. Bake on a silicone baking sheet at 200°C for 30-40 minutes till the "fries" are soft but slightly browned and crispy on the outside. Flip them midway for even browning.
4. Serve with cashew mayonnaise (pg 230).

Juicy Corn with Peanut Podi

Serves 2

Ingredients

- 2 whole corn on the cob, halved
- 2 tbsp peanut chilli garlic chutney (pg 218)
- 1 lemon, cut in half

Method

1. Boil the corn for 5-10 minutes until cooked.
2. Use half a lemon dipped in the peanut chilli garlic chutney and apply on the cob.
3. Serve hot.

Ingredients

For the Garnish

- 6 large lettuce leaves
- 3 tomatoes, sliced
- 2 onions, cut into thin rings
- 3 tbsp pickled jalapeno, sliced

For the Pocket

- 1 cup rolled oats, ground to flour
- 1 cup sweet potato, steamed and mashed
- ¼ cup water
- Salt to taste

For the Filling

- 3 medium eggplants
- 2 tomatoes, finely chopped
- ¾ tsp garlic paste
- ¾ tsp ginger paste
- ½ tsp chilli powder
- 2 onions, finely chopped
- Salt to taste

For Tahini Sauce

- ½ cup tahini paste
- 4 tbsp water
- 2 cloves garlic, crushed
- 1 tbsp lemon juice
- Salt to taste

Chef's Note: *Since sweet potatoes vary in size and variety, you can steam them for 10-15 minutes depending on size, till completely soft. When slightly cooled, mash the sweet potatoes thoroughly with a fork or in a food processor.*

Roasted Eggplant Pita Pocket

Makes 6 halves

Method

1. To prepare the pita pocket, place the sweet potato mash, oats flour and salt in a mixing bowl. Gradually add the water to make a dough by kneading it to a smooth consistency so it is easy to roll.
2. Divide the dough in 3 equal portions. Using your hands, pat each ball to flatten and spread on a silicone sheet or a parchment paper. Smoothen the edges if they break while spreading. Spread the balls into approximately 6 inch wide circles, keeping them thick as we want them to puff up when baked.
3. Bake at 180° C for 30 minutes. When the base is brown and cooked, it will naturally rise. Depending on the oven you may need to cook both sides.
4. Meanwhile, roast the eggplants on an open fire on all sides till the skin is charred and eggplant is soft which should take about 15-20 minutes. Allow it to cool, remove the charred skin and mash the eggplant thoroughly with a fork.
5. In a wok, saute the onions, ginger and garlic for 5 minutes till browned. Sprinkle some water if it sticks to the pan. Add the mashed eggplant, tomato, chilli powder and salt. Continue to stir and cook the mixture for another 15-20 minutes, on medium to low heat, until the whole mixture is reddish brown in colour.
6. Blend together all the tahini sauce ingredients.
7. Slice the cooled pita pocket into half. Run the knife gently inside the slit to create a 'pocket'.
8. Now assemble the filling in the pocket by first lining it with some lettuce on one side. On the other side, place the sliced tomatoes and onion rings.
9. In between fill it with the prepared eggplant. Top it with jalapeno and a generous helping of tahini sauce.
10. Serve immediately or the pita will soften.

Millet Punjabi Panjiri

Serves 6-8

Ingredients

- 1 cup little millets *(sama)*
- 1 cup fox nuts *(makhana)*
- ½ cup desiccated coconut
- ¼ cup edible gum *(gond)*
- 1 cup mixed nuts - almonds, pistachios, cashew nuts
- 2 tbsp melon seeds
- ½ tsp ginger powder
- ¼ tsp white pepper powder
- 3 tbsp dry date powder *(kharek powder)*

Method

1. On medium heat, dry roast while stirring each ingredient in the following order and remove each ingredient from the heat and keep aside one by one:

    a. Millets for 5 minutes
    b. Fox nuts for 3 minutes
    c. Edible gum for 2 minutes, till it changes colour and puffs up.
    d. Mixed nuts for 3-4 minutes, till they release an aroma
    e. Desiccated coconut for 2-3 minutes
    f. Melon seeds for 3-4 minutes, make sure to keep the pan covered as they crackle and split.

2. In a grinder crush the cooled *makhana* and nuts coarsely. Remove into a mixing bowl.
3. Now mix all the ingredients together to make a delicious snack. This can be stored for up to 2-3 weeks in an airtight container.

Time Pass Chiwda

Serves 4

Ingredients

- 1 cup popped amaranth seeds
- ½ cup peanuts, roasted
- ¼ cup pumpkin and sunflower seeds, roasted
- ½ cup curry leaves *(kadi patta)*, roasted
- 2-3 whole dried red chillies, roasted
- 1-2 cloves garlic (optional)
- 1 tbsp raisins, chopped
- Salt to taste

Method

1. In a grinder, make a powder of half the peanuts, garlic (if using), red chillies and salt.
2. Crumble the dried curry leaves with your hands.
3. Mix everything together and toss well to make your healthy, tasty chiwda.

Gooey Elaichi Cookies

Makes 6 pieces

Ingredients

- 1 cup rolled oats, coarsely ground
- 1 cup mixed nuts (almond, cashew, walnuts), roughly crushed
- ½ cup mixed dried fruit (apricots, figs, berries), chopped fine
- 2 tbsp black raisins
- 1 tsp green cardamom, ground
- 4-6 tbsp date paste (pg 232)
- 4 tbsp peanut butter (pg 228)

Method

1. Mix all the ingredients, except the peanut butter, to form a stiff dough. You may adjust the date paste according to desired sweetness.
2. Make 6 round balls in the palm of your hands and flatten them to form cookie size rounds, around 3 inches wide.
3. Lay the cookies on a silicone sheet or parchment paper.
4. Preheat oven to 180°C for 10 minutes and bake the cookies for 30 minutes or till golden brown.
5. When cookies are ready, allow them to cool. Then you can create cookie sandwiches by spreading them with peanut butter filling and enjoy the extra decadent and delicious treat.

Chef's Note: *You can do a lot of variations on this basic recipe by changing the spice to cinnamon, vanilla or nutmeg and using almond or cashew butter. For chocolate cookies, you can use cocoa butter and a tablespoon of cacao powder.*

Golden Badam Thandai

Serves 2

Ingredients

- 2 glasses almond milk (pg 222)
- 12 pods of green cardamom, peeled and crushed
- 4 tbsp date paste (pg 232)
- 5 almonds, finely sliced and toasted
- ½ tsp turmeric powder

Method

1. Blend all the ingredients (expect toasted almonds and a little cardamom) well and pour into glasses.
2. Use ice if you need the drink to be cold.
3. Sprinkle the roasted almonds and a little crushed cardamom on top before serving.

Gulabo Lassi

Serves 2

Ingredients

- 2 glasses thin coconut milk (pg 225)
- 1 tbsp fresh or dried edible rose petals
- 1 tbsp edible rose water *(gulab jal)*
- 1 tsp beetroot juice
- 4 tbsp yellow raisin paste (pg 233)
- 4 ice cubes

Method

1. Blend together ½ the rose petals, raisin paste and a little coconut milk to make a thick paste.
2. Add the remaining ingredients and blend again.
3. Decorate with the remaining rose petals before serving.

Nut-free Citrus Bars

Makes 8

Ingredients

For the Bar

- 1 cup rolled oats
- 1 cup mixed seeds (sunflower, pumpkin, flax, melon, cucumber)
- 6 soft dates, pitted and chopped
- 1 tbsp green raisins
- 3 dried figs, finely chopped
- 2 tbsp black raisins
- 2 tsp orange rind, grated
- 3 tbsp date paste (pg 232)

For the topping

- 1 tbsp cacao nibs
- 1 tbsp sunflower seeds
- 2 tbsp orange rind, julienned finely

Method

1. Put the oats and seeds in a food processor and roughly grind until all seeds and oats are half broken. Add the chopped dates, figs and green raisins and pulse to grind coarsely.
2. Place the mixture in a mixing bowl and add the black raisins, orange rind, and date paste and mix together to form a soft dough
3. Shape the mixture into bars of ¾" height, 1" width and 3-3½" length.
4. Decorate the top of the bars with cacao nibs, sunflower seeds and some orange rind.
5. Bake at 190°C for 15-20 minutes until slightly brown.
6. Allow to cool and then wrap in parchment paper and keep in the fridge as a snack to go. This can stay in the fridge for upto 3 weeks.

Chef's Note: *For the orange rind, take some orange peels and scrape off the white portion completely before cutting into juliennes.*

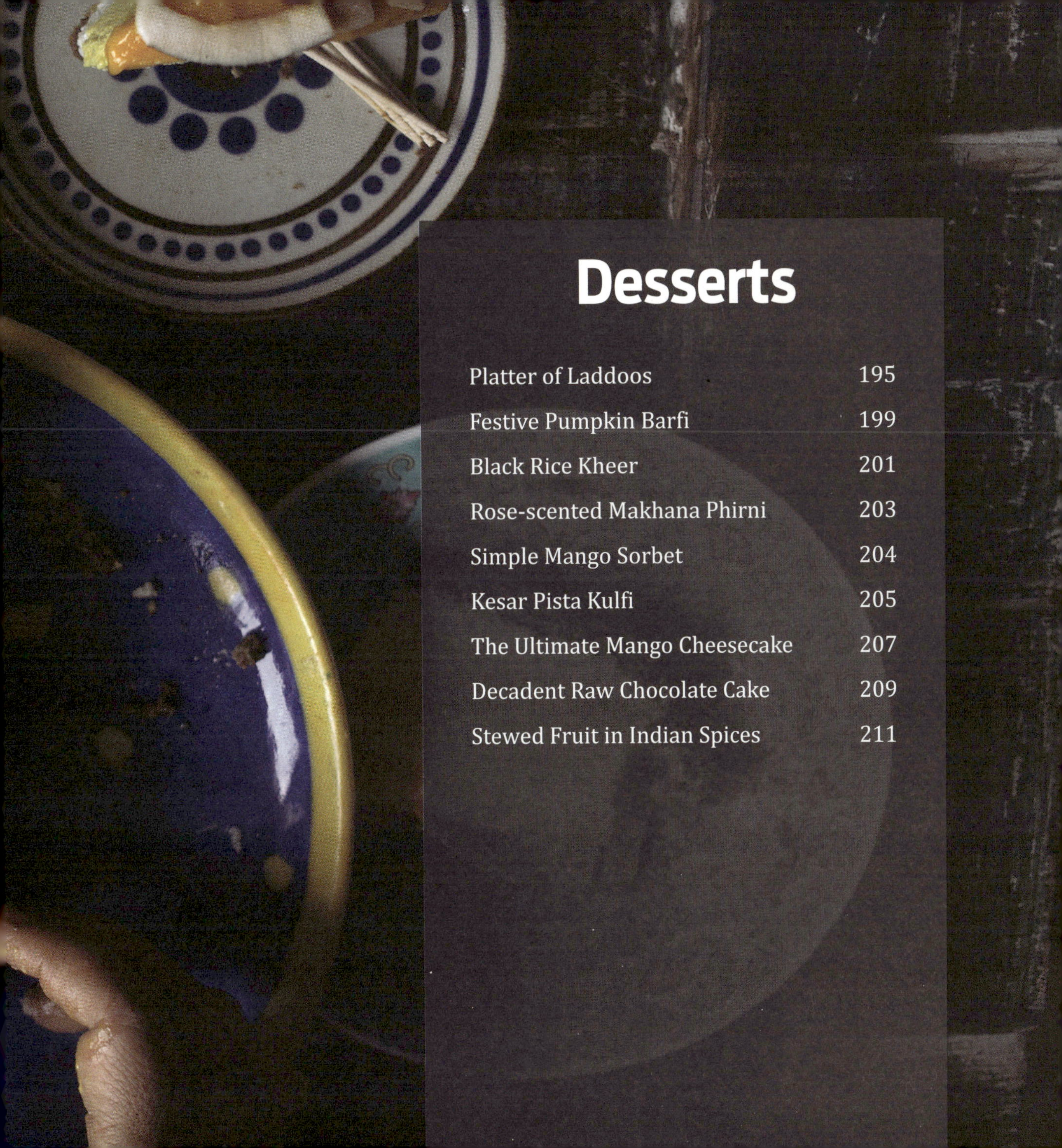

Desserts

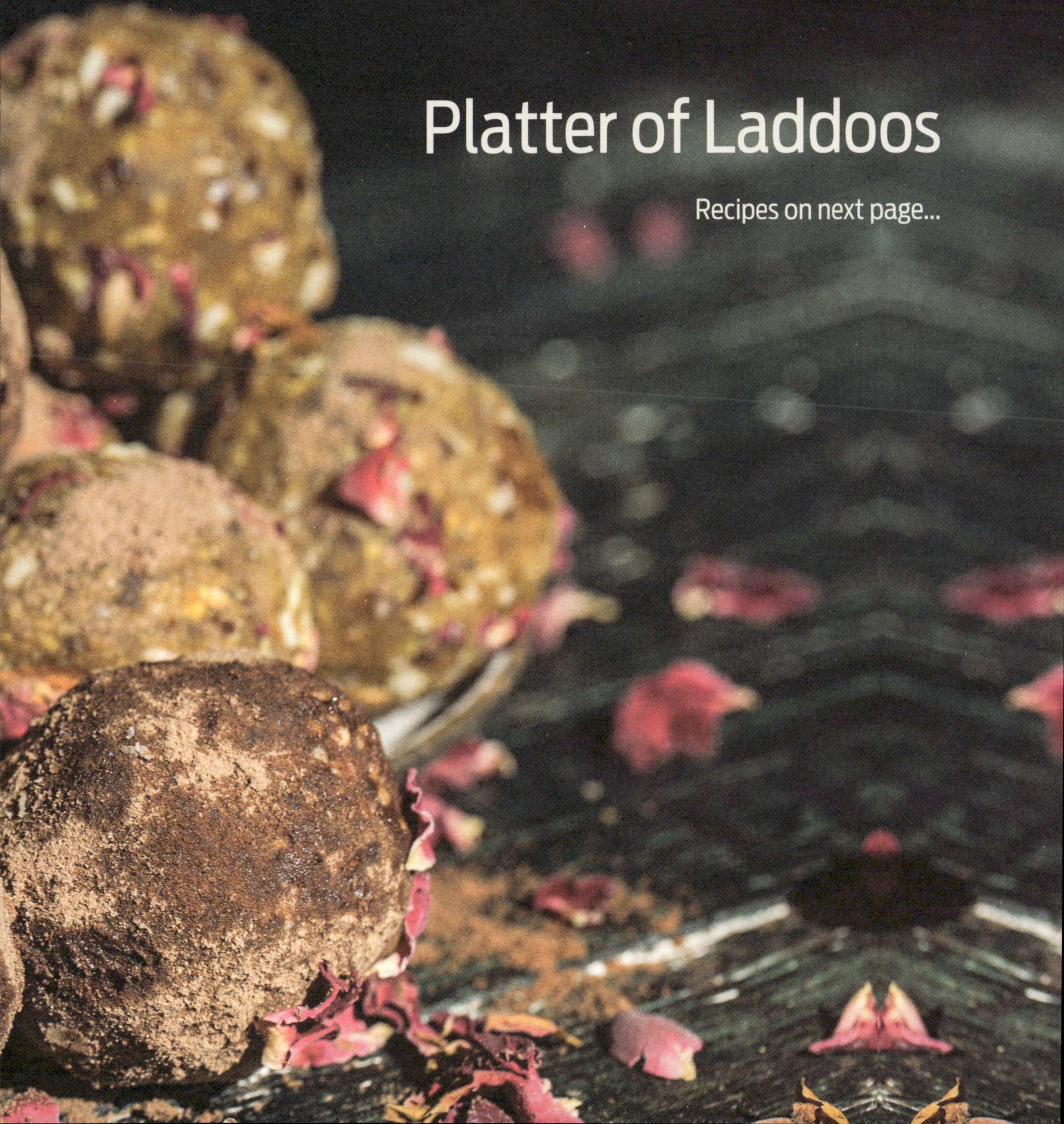

Platter of Laddoos

Recipes on next page...

A) Chocolate Almond Laddo

Makes 8 laddoos

Ingredients

- ½ cup almonds, roasted but unsalted
- ¼ cup soft dates, mashed with a fork
- ½ tsp vanilla powder
- Pinch of salt
- 1½ tbsp cacao powder

Method

1. Grind the roasted almonds to a coarse powder in a food processor.
2. Add in the remaining ingredients, keeping aside ½ tbsp cacao powder, and process to a sticky dough.
3. Form balls or laddoos using your hands and roll them in the remaining cacao powder to coat evenly.
4. Store in fridge to harden. This can be kept in the fridge for up to 2 weeks.

Chef's Note: *Freshly roasted almonds have the best flavour. You can roast them in a wok on low to medium heat, stirring them frequently for 10-12 minutes. You can also roast them in the oven by spreading them on a tray and baking at 180°C for 10 minutes. Use after cooling. The almonds should be crisp and crunchy.*

B) Besan Laddoo

Makes 12 laddoos

Ingredients

- 1 cup split bengal gram lentil *(chana daal)*
- ½ cup fresh coconut, grated
- ½ cup almonds
- 2 cup dates, pitted
- ½ tsp green cardamom *(elaichi)* powder
- ½ cup dried rose petals

Method

1. Roast the *chana daal* in a hot wok for 7-8 minutes on medium heat till it turns golden in colour. Allow to cool and grind it to a fine powder.
2. Transfer to a food processor and add the almonds, cardamom powder, grated coconut and process coarsely.
3. Add the dates and process into a sticky dough.
4. Add the rose petals and pulse for 2-3 seconds to mix in the petals but not shred them.
5. Roll into laddoos. Cool in the refrigerator for a few hours to harden before eating. These can be kept in the refrigerator for up to a week.

C) Coconut Laddoo

Makes 8 laddoos

Ingredients

- 2 ¼ cups fresh coconut, scraped or finely grated
- ½ cup soft dates, pitted and mashed with a fork

Method

1. Roast the grated coconut in a hot wok on medium heat for 10-12 minutes till lightly browned. Keep stirring frequently to avoid burning. Allow it to cool.
2. Mix in the mashed dates with the cooled coconut leaving aside ¼ cup of coconut for final coating.
3. Form small-sized balls by rolling between your hands.
4. To coat, spread the remaining coconut on a plate and roll the balls in it making sure they are evenly coated.

Chef's Note: *We used 8 soft dates that mashed into ½ cup. Adjust according to the size of the dates available to you.*

Festive Pumpkin Barfi

Makes 10-12 pieces

Ingredients

For the Barfi

- 2 cups gram flour *(besan)*
- ¼ cup yellow pumpkin, finely shredded
- ¼ cup sweet yellow raisin paste (pg 233)
- ¼ cup date paste (pg 232)
- 1/2 tsp green cardamom *(elaichi)* powder
- ¼ cup green pumpkin seeds

Method

1. Dry roast the *besan* in a hot wok on low to medium heat for approximately 15-20 minutes until you can smell the aroma. Keep stirring constantly to avoid burning. Remove from heat and allow to cool.
2. Squeeze the water out of the shredded pumpkin and discard. Mix the pumpkin into the *besan* using your hands, coating the pumpkin evenly.
3. Add the two pastes gradually using enough to form a firm dough.
4. Add the cardamom and spread the dough 1" in height on a flat dish.
5. Place in the refrigerator uncovered overnight to firm up further.
6. Next morning cut the barfi into diamond shapes and garnish with green pumpkin seeds.

Chef's Note*: Do not cook the besan on high heat as the colour will darken due to burning. The reason for using two sweeteners is that raisins can be sour. However using only dates will darken the barfi. Yellow raisins are usually less sour than darker varieties plus they help to preserve the colour. Try to find the sweetest yellow raisins with least amount of sourness.*

Black Rice Kheer

Serves 6

Ingredients

- 1 cup black rice
- 2 cups almond milk (pg 222)
- 2 tbsp crushed almonds
- 1 ½ cup date paste (pg 232)
- 1 tsp green cardamom *(elaichi)*, crushed

Method

1. Wash and soak the black rice in 2 cups of water for 3-4 hours.
2. Cook the rice in the soaking water for 10 minutes.
3. Add in the almond milk, stir and cook the mixture for another 5 minutes till rice is soft. Turn off the heat.
4. Add the crushed almonds, date paste and cardamom and mix thoroughly. Check the sweetness and adjust according to taste.
5. Serve hot or cold.

Rose-scented Makhana Phirni

Serves 4

Ingredients

- 2 cups fox nuts *(makhana)*, ground into flour
- ½ cup almond milk (pg 222)
- ½ cup dry date *(kharek)* powder or sweet yellow raisin paste (pg 233)
- ½ tsp green cardamom, crushed
- A few fresh or dried rose petals for garnish

Method

1. In a wok roast the fox nut flour on medium heat for 5-7 minutes till slightly brown. Keep stirring continuously to avoid burning.
2. Add the almond milk, *kharek* powder or raisin paste and crushed cardamom. Cook for approximately 5 minutes on high heat.
3. Remove from heat and allow the mixture to cool.
4. This dessert can be eaten warm or cold. If you want to eat it cold then place it in individual bowls and leave in the fridge to chill.
5. Garnish with the rose petals before serving.

Chef's Note: *Please ensure that the raisins are not at all sour or it will make your phirni taste sour. If you cannot get sweet yellow raisins, then use dry date (kharek) powder or date paste (pg 236) although date paste will darken the colour of the phirni.*

Simple Mango Sorbet

Serves 4-6

Ingredients

- 2 ripe mangoes
- 2 tbsp coconut cream (pg 226)

Method

1. Scoop and blend the flesh of the mangoes until smooth.
2. Freeze the pulp overnight in a container. This can stay for up to 1 month in the freezer.
3. To serve, take out from the freezer and allow the sorbet to become a little soft so that the scoops can be formed with an ice cream scooper.
4. It has to be served immediately or else the scoops will lose shape.
5. Drizzle some coconut cream when serving.

Kesar Pista Kulfi

Serves 4-6

Ingredients

- 1 cup thick almond milk (pg 222)
- ½ cup pistachios, shelled and roughly crushed
- 6 strands saffron
- ½ cup raisin paste (pg 233)

For Garnishing

- 2 tbsp pistachio flakes
- 6 strands of saffron

Method

1. Mix all ingredients together except garnishing.
2. Pour into *kulfi* moulds or in small size shot glasses and freeze overnight.
3. Sprinkle the pistachio flakes and saffron strands before serving.

The Ultimate Mango Cheesecake

Serves 8-10

Ingredients

For the Crust

- 1 cup almonds
- ½ cup soft dates, pitted
- 2 tbsp flaxseed, powdered
- Pinch of salt

For the Filling

- 1½ cups cashews, soaked for 4 hours
- 3 cups ripe mango, cut into chunks
- 1 cup thick coconut cream (pg 226)
- 1 cup yellow raisin paste (pg 233)

For the Garnish (optional)

- 1 cup cherries
- ½ cup dried coconut slices

Method

1. Pulse the almonds in a food processor until you get a coarse powder. Add the remaining crust ingredients and pulse again. The mixture should stick together when pressed and moulded. If too dry, add more dates to make it sticky.
2. Take a 6" springform pan and press the mixture firmly into the bottom and even out the surface. Set in the freezer while you do the next steps.
3. Blend ½ cup soaked cashews with ½ cup raisin paste till smooth. Spread over the crust of the cheesecake and put it back in the freezer to set for 30 minutes.
4. Blend the remaining cashews and raisins with the coconut cream. When smooth, add 2 cups of mangoes and blend again till smooth.
5. Pour this filling over the cashew layer and put into the freezer for 1-2 hours to set.
6. For the top layer of the cheesecake, blend the remaining mango into a smooth purée. You can add some soaked raisins if the mango is not sweet enough. Finish with spreading this as the top layer and freeze again for minimum 3 hours before eating.
7. Decorate with cherries and dried coconut slices on top before serving (optional). You can also use chopped mangoes or any other fruit to decorate. The cheesecake can be stored without the garnish for up to 10 days in the freezer. Just thaw for 20-30 minutes before eating.

Chef's Tip: *If you want to cut preparation time, just make the bottom crust and then blend all the filling ingredients together and freeze instead of doing 3 different coloured layers.*

Decadent Raw Chocolate Cake

Serves 6

Ingredients

For the Cake

- 1 cup bitter almonds, ground into flour
- 1 cup date paste (pg 232)
- ¼ cup cacao powder
- 1 tsp pure vanilla powder
- 1 tbsp lime juice
- Dash of ground black pepper
- Pinch of salt

For the Topping

- ½ cup cashews, soaked for 4-6 hours
- 2 tbsp raisin paste (pg 233)
- ½ tsp pure vanilla powder
- 1 tbsp cacao powder

Method

1. Add all the cake ingredients to the almond flour and process to a thick and gooey mixture.
2. In a small spring form pan, press the mixture down tight and smoothen the top with the back of a large spoon to flatten. Chill in the freezer while you assemble the topping.
3. Drain the water from cashews. Grind all the topping ingredients together using a little water if necessary to move the blades.
4. Pull out the cake from the freezer and spread this thick cashew cream on top evenly. Allow it to chill again in the freezer for 4-6 hours. Even if it freezes for longer, you can thaw for 15-30 minutes before eating.
5. Before serving, you can decorate the top with any seasonal fruit of your liking or sprinkle the cacao powder.

Chef's Note: *You can use regular almonds if bitter almonds are not available but the latter give a lovely and unique flavour to this cake.*

Stewed Fruit in Indian Spices

Serves 4

Ingredients

- 2 cups of mixed fresh fruit chopped into large pieces (pineapple, pear, apple)
- 6 whole figs
- 4 whole dates
- 4 whole prunes
- 2 pieces star anise
- 4 cloves
- A few cherries for garnishing

Method

1. Place the figs, star anise and cloves in ¼ cup water in a pan. Cover with a lid and cook on medium heat for about 5-7 minutes allowing the figs to soften and puff up.
2. Add the fresh fruit and cook for approximately 5 minutes on medium heat making sure the fruit does not overcook.
3. Add the dates and prunes and cook fo another 2-3 minutes. Be careful of overcooking as the fruit can easily disintegrate. There should also be some natural syrup formed from the juices of the fruit.
4. Garnish with some cherries, drizzle with the natural syrup and serve hot or cold.

CHUTNEYS

WET

DRY

Fresh Coconut Chutney

Makes 1 cup

Ingredients

- 2 cups coconut, grated
- ½ green chilli, broken
- 2 tbsp split bengal gram lentil *(chana daal)*
- 1 tsp black mustard seeds
- 6-8 fresh or dried curry leaves *(kadi patta)*
- 1 dried red chilli, broken into 3-4 pieces
- Salt to taste

Method

1. Dry roast the *chana daal* for 2-3 minutes till it emits an aroma. Cool and grind coarsely.
2. Add grated coconut, green chilli, salt and ¼- ½ cup water as needed to move the blades and grind coarsely.
3. For the tempering, on medium heat roast the mustard seeds, red chilli and curry leaves until mustard seeds pop.
4. Mix the coconut mixture and the tempering together and serve.

Classic Green Chutney

Makes 3/4 cu

Ingredients

- 1½ cups fresh coriander leaves and soft stems, chopped and tightly packed
- ½ cup mint leaves, tightly packed
- ¼ tsp cumin powder
- ½tsp ginger, grated
- ½ green chilli, broken
- 2 tbsp lemon juice
- 1 tbsp raisin paste (pg 233)
- Salt to taste

Method

1. Blend all the ingredients together with ¼ cup water to make a smooth paste.
2. Serve as an accompaniment to any main dish.

Sweet Ambol Chutney

Makes 11/2 cup

Ingredients

- 4 ripe tomatoes, cut into large chunks
- 1 tsp *panch phoran* spice - equal proportion of fennel seed *(saunf)*, cumin seed *(jeera)*, onion seed *(kalonji)*, mustard seed and a pinch of asafoetida *(heeng)*, combined together.
- 2 dried red chillies, broken
- ½ cup onion, chopped
- 6 tbsp date paste (pg 232)
- Salt to taste

Method

1. Dry rost the *panch phoran* and red chillies for 2-3 minutes on medium heat till they emit an aroma.
2. Add the chopped onions. Cover and cook for 4-5 minutes till the onions are transparent but not brown. Sprinkle a little water to avoid burning and sticking to the pan.
3. Add the chopped tomatoes and salt and stir and cook covered for 4-5 minutes until soft and squishy. Smash the tomatoes with the back of a spoon keeping the sauce a little chunky.
4. Add the date paste and cook further for 1-2 minutes.
5. Remove from heat and serve cold.

***Chef's Note:** For the panch phoran, you can make a larger batch and store in an airtight container to use later.*

Poshto Chutney

Makes 3/4 cup

Ingredients

- ½ cup white poppy seeds
- ¾ cup tomatoes, roughly chopped
- 1 dried red chilli
- Salt to taste

Method

1. In a small wok or *kadhai*, roast the chilli and poppy seeds for 3-4 minutes till poppy seeds are slightly brown.
2. Cool and grind together.
3. Add the tomatoes, salt and 2 tbsp water if required to move the blades and grind again until a smooth and thick paste is formed. Serve fresh.

Easy Tamarind Chutney

Makes 1/2 cup

Ingredients

- ¼ cup date paste (pg 232)
- ¼ cup tamarind paste (pg 234)
- Pinch of asafoetida *(heeng)*
- 1 tsp ginger, grated
- Pinch of red chilli powder (optional)
- Salt to taste

Method

1. Blend all the ingredients together to make a smooth paste. Use a little water if needed to bring it to the desired consistency.
2. Serve as an accompaniment to any main dish.

Peanut Chilli Garlic Chutney

Makes 1 cup

Ingredients

- ¾ cup peanuts, roasted
- 2 dried red chillies
- 2-3 cloves garlic, chopped
- Salt to taste

Method

1. Roast the chillies in a small pan for 2-3 minutes. Cool to crisp.
2. Break the chillies and grind together all the ingredients to make a coarse powder.
3. Serve as an accompaniment to any Indian meal.

Chef's Note: *This can be stored for 1 month in an airtight container.*

Flaxseed Tamarind Chutney

Makes 1 cup

Ingredients

- ¾ cup flaxseed, raw or roasted depending on the taste you prefer
- 1-2 dried red chillies
- 1 tbsp dry tamarind, seeds and strings removed
- Salt to taste

Method

1. Roast the chillies in a small pan for 2-3 minutes. Cool to crisp.
2. Break the chillies and grind together all the ingredients to make a coarse powder.
3. Serve as an accompaniment to any Indian meal.

Chef's Note: *If using raw flaxseeds, this can be stored in the refrigerator for 1 week. If using roasted flaxseeds, the chutney can be stored for 2 weeks.*

Sesame Fenugreek Chutney

Makes 1 cup

Ingredients

- ½ cup white, unpolished sesame seeds *(safed til)*
- 2 dried red chillies
- 1 tbsp dried fenugreek leaves *(kasoori methi)*
- 1 clove garlic (optional)
- Salt to taste

Method

1. Roast the sesame seeds in a wok on medium heat for 6-8 minutes till slightly browned. Cool completely.
2. Roast the chillies in a small pan for 2-3 minutes. Cool to crisp.
3. Break the chillies and grind together all the ingredients to make a coarse powder.
4. Serve as an accompaniment to any dish.

Chef's Note: *This can be stored in an airtight container in the refrigerator for up to 2 weeks.*

Dessicated Coconut Chutney

Makes 11/2 cup

Ingredients

- 1 cup dry grated or dessicated coconut
- 2 tbsp dehusked black gram lentil *(dhuli urad daal)*
- ¼ cup packed fresh curry leaves *(kadi patta)*
- 1 tbsp white, unpolished sesame seeds *(safed til)*
- 1-2 dried red chillies
- Pinch of asafoetida *(heeng)*
- 1 tsp tamarind, seeds and strings removed
- Salt to taste

Method

1. Roast the coconut in a wok on medium heat for 5-7 minutes, stirring continuously till it emits an aroma.
2. Roast the *daal* separately for 2-3 minutes on medium flame. When half done, add the red chillies, sesame and curry leaves and stir and roast for another 2-3 minutes.
3. Break the chillies, add the remaining ingredients and grind together to make a coarse powder.
4. Serve as an accompaniment to any meal.

Chef's Note: *This can be stored in an airtight container in the refrigerator for 1 week.*

BASIC RECIPES

Almond Milk

Makes 1 litre

Ingredients

- 1 cup raw almonds
- 1 litre water

Method

1. Soak the almonds for minimum 6 hours or up to overnight.
2. Discard the soaking water and add 1½ cups water, from the 1 litre water.
3. Blend into a very smooth paste.
4. Add the remaining water and blend again.

Chef's Note: *Almond milk can substitute milk requirement in smoothies, kheers, with cereal or in conventional recipes. To get smoother milk, especially for children, you can strain the milk through a muslin cloth or nut milk bag and add the remaining fibre to curries, vegetables, soups or dough. Almond milk can stay in the fridge for 2-3 days.*

Peanut Curd With Fibre

Makes 1 litre

Ingredients

- 1 cup raw peanuts
- 1 litre water
- 10-12 green chilli crowns

Method

1. Soak the peanuts for 6 hours covering them completely with water.
2. Discard the water used for soaking.
3. Using 1.5 cups of the 1 litre water, grind the peanuts thoroughly to a fine paste in a blender.
4. Add the remaining water and blend again for 1-2 minutes to get a smooth milk.
5. Boil the peanut milk in a pan on medium heat and stir intermittently till it comes to a boil. Now lower the heat to simmer and stir continuously for 5-7 minutes to prevent sticking and burning at the bottom.
6. Remove from the heat and allow to cool down to lukewarm temperature for setting the curd.
7. Add the crowns of the green chillies to the lukewarm milk. Mix thoroughly.
8. Leave the milk covered and undisturbed in a dark corner or cupboard for 8-10 hours in the summer or 12-15 hours during winter. You can check if the curd is set by scooping out a little with a spoon. It should be thick and set.

Chef's Note: *Chilli crowns provide the probiotics required for setting curd so it is a completely plant-based starter. If available, you can use 3 tbsp of vegan curd as a starter. For the next batch, use the culture from this batch of curd. The starter can be stored for up to a week in the fridge or up to 3 months in the freezer.*

Rice and Peanut Curd

Makes 1 litre

Ingredients

- 1 cup raw peanuts
- ¼ cup unpolished brown or red rice
- 1 tbsp lime juice
- 6-8 green chilli crowns
- 1 litre water

Method

1. Soak the peanuts and rice together for 8 hours covering them completely with water.
2. Discard the water used for soaking.
3. Using 1.5 cups of the 1 litre water, grind the rice and peanuts thoroughly to a fine paste in a blender.
4. Now add the remaining water and blend again for 1-2 minutes.
5. Use a muslin cloth or nut milk bag to strain the liquid into a pan and discard the left over fibre.
6. Boil the milk in a pan on medium heat and stir intermittently till it comes to a boil. Now lower the heat to simmer and stir continuously for 5-7 minutes to prevent sticking and burning at the bottom. The milk will thicken as the rice gets cooked.
7. Remove from the heat and allow to cool down to lukewarm temperature for setting curd.
8. Add the lime juice and green chilli crowns. Mix thoroughly.
9. Leave it covered and undisturbed in a dark corner or cupboard for 8-10 hours in the summer or 12-15 hours during winter. You can check if the curd is set by scooping out a little with a spoon. It should be thick and set.

Chef's Note: *Chilli crowns provide the probiotics required for setting curd so it is a completely plant based starter. If available, you can also use 3 tbsp of vegan curd as a starter. For the next batch, use the culture from this batch of curd. It can be stored for up to a week in the fridge or up to 3 months in the freezer.*

Coconut Milk (Thin and Thick)

Makes 2 cups thick milk and 1 cup thin milk

Ingredients

- 1 cup mature brown coconut, shredded
- 2 cups water (for thick milk)
- Additional 1 cup water (for thin milk)

Method

1. For thick milk, blend the shredded coconut with 1 cup water to a smooth paste. Add the remaining water and blend again.
2. Using a muslin cloth or nut milk bag, remove the fibre. This will yield thick milk.
3. For thin milk, use the same fibre. Put it back in the blender with 1 cup water and blend again. Remove the fibre through the cloth again to yield thin milk.
4. For medium-thick milk, mix the above two to yield 3 cups.

Chef's Note: *Coconut milk is not completely wholesome as the fibre has been removed. It is to be used sparingly especially if reversing a medical condition. Yet, it is an excellent and more nutritious substitute for regular milk.*

Since we eat coconuts raw, this milk does not need to be boiled but it can be heated for a recipe. You can adjust the thickness of the coconut milk by adding more or less water. Do it a few times and you will be an expert.

Coconut Cream

Makes 250ml

Ingredients

- 1 cup mature brown coconut, shredded
- 200ml water

Method

1. Blend the shredded coconut in half the water to a smooth paste. Add the remaining water and blend again.
2. Using a muslin cloth or nut milk cloth, remove the fibre.
3. Refrigerate the cream for minimum 4 hours and up to 12 hours to further thicken the consistency.

Chef's Note: *This is a good substitute to dairy cream e.g. use for garnishing daal, vegetables, soups etc. Use it sparingly, especially if reversing a health condition.*

Coconut Butter

Makes ½ cup

Ingredients

- 1 cup mature brown coconut, shredded
- 200ml water

Method

1. Blend the shredded coconut in half the water to a smooth paste. Add the remaining water and blend again.
2. Using a muslin cloth or nut milk cloth, remove the fibre.
3. Refrigerate the cream for 24-36 hours without disturbing it.
4. A thick layer will form on top separating the water at the bottom.
5. Carefully scoop out the thick hardened cream and use it as butter.

Chef's Note: *Use the butter as a substitute to dairy butter, on chapatis, to flavor soups and lentils as needed. If you are reversing a medical condition or intending to shed excess weight, then consume sparingly or not at all as this is high in fat. Yet, it is far more nutritious and cholesterol-free compared to regular butter.*

Peanut Butter

Makes ½ cup

Ingredients

- 1 cup peanuts, roasted and unsalted

Method

1. In a small dry grinder, powder the peanuts. Keep pulsing and grinding for a few minutes. Scrape any peanuts stuck to the sides and pulse again.
2. The peanuts will first turn to powder, then become sticky and if you keep going, eventually it will release oil and become buttery.

Chef's Note: *Use this butter to substitute fat in many dishes. It can be used to make salad dressings, spread on chapati or toast or substitute butter in baking recipes. To make it even tastier, at the time of grinding you can add 1 pitted date and ½ tsp salt to get a sweet and salty taste.*

You can also make any seed or nut butter using the same recipe e.g. almond butter, pumpkin seed butter, cashew butter, walnut butter, sesame seed butter or tahini etc.

Cashew Cream (Plain, Sweet or Savoury)

Makes 1 cup plain or savoury or 1½ cups sweet

Ingredients

- ½ cup cashews
- 1 cup water

For Savoury

- 1 tsp garlic, minced
- 1 tbsp lime juice
- Salt to taste

For Sweet

- ¼ cup raisins, soaked in ¼ cup water for 4 hours

Method

1. Soak the cashews for 4-6 hours.
2. Grind the cashews for a plain cashew cream.
3. Grind the cashews and savoury ingredients for savoury cashew cream.
4. Grind the cashews and soaked raisins for the sweet cashew cream.

Chef's Note: *Use the savoury cream to add the fat needed to lift any savoury dish like vegetables or soup. It can also be used as a salad dressing or sandwich spread.*

The sweet cream can be used as garnish for fruits or desserts as indicated in a recipe.

These can last in the refrigerator for 2-3 days.

Cashew Mayonnaise

Makes 1 cup

Ingredients

- ½ cup cashews
- 1 cup water
- ¼ tsp mustard powder
- ½ tsp garlic, minced
- 2 tbsp onions, chopped
- Salt to taste

Method

1. Soak the cashews for 4-6 hours in the water.
2. Discard the soaking water and grind all the ingredients together to a smooth paste adding a little water as needed to yield a mayonnaise-like consistency.

Chef's Note: *Soaking makes a smooth paste. In an emergency, you can grind the cashews to a powder and then add the remaining ingredients. However, in that case the yield maybe a little grainy.*

Can be used as a sandwich spread or dipping sauce to substitute regular mayonnaise. This can last in the refrigerator for 3 days.

Cashew Cheese

Makes approximately 1½ cups

Ingredients

- ½ cup cashews
- 1 cup water
- ½ tsp garlic, minced
- 1 tbsp lime juice
- Salt to taste
- Black pepper to taste

Method

1. Soak the cashews in the water for 4-6 hours.
2. Grind to a very smooth paste and allow it to sit overnight in a glass jar with a loose fitting lid.
3. The cashew cheese should rise and smell a little off but not unpalatable, just like cheese. It should also have little air pockets where the bacteria have caused fermentation. Then you know it is ready.
4. The surface should be white. If it turns pink, then fungus has started growing on it. If this happens, you can carefully scrape off the pink parts and use the rest.
5. This is the basic cheese. Into this you can mix the remaining ingredients or any other flavours you like.

Chef's Note: *Use as a sandwich spread, on pasta, pizza or as a dip with vegetable sticks. It can substitute cream cheese in conventional recipes.*

Date Paste

Makes 1 cup

Ingredients

- 1 cup soft dates, pitted, packed
- 1 cup water

Method

1. Soak the dates in the given water for 1-2 hours. If the dates are hard, you may need to soak longer.
2. Grind the dates using as little of the soaking water as necessary to grind to a smooth paste. Adjust thickness by adding more water if needed.

Chef's Note: *Dates can substitute sugar in most recipes. There are many varieties available with different levels of softness, size and texture. Use the ones most convenient for you.*

Due to their dark colour, dates will darken any white desserts but everywhere else, they are the best alternative to sugar. Date paste can stay in the refrigerator for up to 1 week and in the freezer for 3 weeks. If kept frozen, thaw before using.

Raisin Paste

Makes ½ cup

Ingredients

- ½ cup raisins
- ⅓ cup water

Method

1. Soak the raisins for 4-6 hours.
2. Grind them using as little of the soaking water as necessary to make a smooth paste.

Chef's Note: *We prefer to use sweet yellow raisins as they are less sour. If using in a sweet dessert, please ensure raisins are not sour. Raisin paste can stay in the refrigerator for 5 days.*

Tamarind Paste

Makes 3/4 cup

Ingredients

- ½ cup tamarind
- ½ cup water

Method

1. Soak the tamarind for 4-6 hours. If short on time, you can soak it in hot water and leave it for 30 minutes.
2. Using the back of a spoon or your hands, rub off the tamarind pulp from the seeds and fibre into the water. Then push the whole mixture through a sieve to yield a smooth and thick paste.

Chef's Note: *Tamarind is a souring agent and can be used instead of lime juice if needed. It has a musky flavour which adds a lovely dimension to the dish. It can be eaten without cooking. You can use it in recipes for salad dressings. This can stay in the refrigerator for 2-3 days.*

GRATITUDE

We are filled with gratitude to the following people for believing in us and unconditionally supporting our work.

Mr. Anil Narang, for his unrelenting support and dedication to the cause of veganism.

Ajai Lakhanpal, for his unconditional and generous support in hosting us at his beautiful property, Aashyana Lakhanpal, Goa where we shot this book.

Our friends, colleagues and clients who tested the recipes and provided valuable feedback - Jinal Rathod, Kajal Shah, Lavleen Riar, Mayavi Khandelwal, Mona Bhardwaj, P.V. Narayanamoorthy, Pooja Gupta and Rosemary Parambi.

Mr. Naresh Mishra, for burning the midnight oil with us while designing this book.

Ms. Mukti Agarwal, for editing out the chinks in the text.

Our families and friends, for constantly encouraging us and for giving us honest feedback.

RESOURCES

To further support your journey into a plant-based diet and lifestyle, we recommend the following films and books. They provide the scientific proof and case study evidence of the health, environmental and spiritual benefits of a plant-based diet.

Documentary Films

What the Health (Health)
Forks over Knives (Health)
May I be Frank (Health)
The Game Changers (Sports and Fitness)
Cowspiracy – The Sustainability Secret (Environment)
Dominion (Animals)
Earthlings (Animals)
A Prayer for Compassion (Spirituality)

Most of these films are available on Netflix or YouTube

Books

How Not to Die by Dr. Michael Greger, M.D.
The China Study by T. Colin Campbell
Undo it by Dr. Dean Ornish, M.D. and Anne Ornish
The Starch Solution by Dr. John McDougall, M.D.
Eat to Live by Dr. Joel Fuhrman, M.D.
Disease Proof Your Child by Dr. Joel Fuhrman, M.D.
Reversing Diabetes by Dr. Neal Barnard, M.D.
Prevent and Reverse Heart Disease by Dr. Caldwell Esselstyn, M.D.
Healthy at 100 by John Robbins

You can also search for the video lectures by these authors on YouTube.